The King in Jeopardy

by
Three-time U.S. Champion
GM Lev Alburt
and
GM Sam Palatnik

Published by:

Chess Information and Research Center
P.O. Box 534
Gracie Station
New York, NY 10028

For ordering information, see page 256.

Distribution to the book trade by:
W.W. Norton, 500 Fifth Avenue, New York, NY

Second, revised edition editing: OutExcel! Corp.,
    Al Lawrence, President
Editor: Mark Ishee
Editorial Advisers: Eric C. Johnson, Bleys Rose
Special Editorial Consultant: Roman Pelts
Translator: Olga Palatnik
Proofreaders: Andrew Mongin, Kent Meadows,
    Peter Kurzdorfer
Typography: JM Productions
Cover: Mark Kostabi's painting, "The King in Jeopardy"
Art Consultant: Lev Maximov
Drawings: Patricia Melvin

ISBN 1-889323-13-6

Library of Congress Catalog Card Number: 98-87726

10 9 8 7 6 5 4 3 2

Printed in the United States of America.

Contents

Part I:
The King in the Center

Lesson One:

Lesson Two:
When the King is Safe in the Center 77

Part II:
Attacks with Same-Side Castling

Lesson Three:
Piece Attacks with Same-Side Castling 97

Part III:
Attacks with Opposite-Side Castling

Foreword

This revised, second edition of *The King in Jeopardy* has been completely re-edited and corrected. Although the pagination of the previous edition was retained, each and every page was re-typeset and re-plated for this new printing.

Ironically, testimony to the timelessness of this book's material is given by an updated example, exercise 9 on page 191, Kramnik—Kasparov, Novgorod, 1997. Kramnik's brilliant move that starts a winning combination against the world champion owes its conception to the more than a century and a half of attacking theory and practice reviewed in this book. GM Kramnik himself acknowledged his debt to the never-out-of-date cornerstones of attacking chess when he remarked after the game, "Back in my childhood I was taught that such a (winning) motif is called *overloading*."

The King in Jeopardy is the fourth volume in the six-volume *Comprehensive Chess Course* series. This book assumes that the reader is familiar with the rules of chess. While it can also stand alone, this book builds on the basic chess concepts and tactical ideas outlined in the previous volumes of the *Course*.

The *Comprehensive Chess Course* originated in the former Soviet Union as a means of providing students with the most effective chess training. Thousands of masters and grandmasters were raised on this course of study. The *Comprehensive Chess Course* is based on the method of repeatedly presenting certain problems to students. The problems become progressively more difficult, combining new ideas with familiar ones, thereby broadening the student's knowledge and simultaneously reinforcing previously mastered material.

Like all the other volumes in the *Course*, *The King in Jeopardy* is designed to be an ideal self-study guide. All the ideas are thoroughly explained.

We wish to take this opportunity to acknowledge our heavy debt to FM Roman Pelts, our special editorial consultant. In addition our editorial advisers—Eric Johnson, Larry Parr, and Bleys Rose—provided a lot of useful criticism and ideas for improvements, for which we are grateful.

Important help was also received from Mark Ishee, while Lev Alburt's students Dr. Martin Katahn and Greg Neu provided useful advice on how to make this book user-friendly for novices and non-masters.

In preparing and marketing this second, revised edition of *The King in Jeopardy*, we've been fortunate to be assisted by Al Lawrence, formerly Executive Director of the US Chess Federation, and now President of OutExcel! Corporation. Al, who promoted USCF's sales and membership to record highs, stays active in the world of chess. He's co-authored three books, *Chess for Children, Winning Chess: Piece by Piece*, and (with GM Lev Alburt) *Playing Computer Chess: Sharpening Your Game*, all from Sterling Press, available from the US Chess Federation and on the internet at www.chesscafe.com. This website offers book reviews, photos, chess want ads, and general and technical articles by leading chess thinkers from around the world.

— GMs Lev Alburt and Sam Palatnik
New York City
October 15, 1998

Introduction

Every chess player, even one who has just taken his first steps in chess, becomes very inspired when he has a chance to make threats directly against the opponent's king. Sometimes even the opportunity simply to make a move that gives check brings joy to the beginner! This reaction is easy to understand, since the goal of the game is to checkmate the king.

When threats to the enemy king are created, sharp positions often occur. Sometimes these positions are full of chances to play beautiful combinations—one of the major reasons players are attracted to chess.

Problems connected with making an attack on the king necessarily occupy an important place in the theory of the middlegame. It is important for players of all strengths to be able to storm the opponent's king effectively, and this is the subject of our book.

Because the attack on the king often involves various kinds of typical combinations and sacrifices, we also recommend that our readers familiarize themselves with various tactical devices by reading the previous book in this series, *Chess Tactics for the Tournament Player*.

Among the many factors that go into evaluating any position, the relative positions of the kings are among the most important. By analyzing numerous examples, we will determine the important characteristics of each major category of positions, and we will also explain typical plans and methods for attack and defense.

Because chess skill is gained primarily through repetition, we have included sets of exercises at the end of each major section of the book. We strongly encourage our readers to work through these exercises with a chess set, taking notes and reaching a general conclusion about each position before going on to the solutions page. At first the exercises may present quite a challenge, but the reader will soon notice an improvement in spotting the correct line of play, as well as in his or her overall thinking style. Time spent on the exercises (and the examples in the text) will soon translate into better understanding during one's own tournament games, and into better results.

Our discussion is intended to be of direct practical benefit. Along the way we will make generalizations and conclusions, all of which are intended to give the readers the necessary experience and knowledge to allow them to navigate the choppy waters of tournament play. Our hope is that where our readers were formerly uncertain or hesitant, they will come to believe in their ability to attack as well as to defend. We hope that our readers, once armed with these new skills, will then use their creative potential to greater effect in the future.

Part I:

The King in the Center

Lesson One

Attacking the King in the Center

In most cases, the chess struggle begins in the center of the board, not on the flanks. Each player starts by trying to obtain dominance in the center by occupying one or more of the central squares — d4, d5, e4, e5. These squares are commonly called "the center" in chess literature. Control of the center, and of the neighboring squares within the rectangle enclosing c3, c6, f6 and f3 (known as the expanded or widened center) allows greater maneuverability and coordination among the pieces, and lays the foundation for a successful attack on the king.

When we refer to an attack on the king in the center, we do not literally mean that the king is in the center of the board on d4, d5, e4 or e5, but that he has remained uncastled and is still on his initial square or on a nearby square on one of the central files. As we shall see, this placement of the king may prove to be quite fraught with danger in the middle game, or even during the transition from opening to the middle game.

The clash of pawns in the center creates tension, and an exchange is likely to occur. Such an exchange will lead to the opening of one or more files or diagonals, which in turn allows pieces to achieve greater activity. If the opponent's king is still in the center and one's forces can be aimed in his direction, the road is now open for an attack. Defense may prove difficult, because without castling the defender's rooks are disconnected and cannot easily be brought to the aid of the king.

If there are open files in the center, these can be a highway for the attacking pieces. A piece which is in the center of the board enjoys greater freedom of action and has more options. This is especially true of knights, which travel more slowly than the bishop, rook, or queen. So when the enemy king sits on the central files, he is an easier target for an attack.

This is not to say that a king in the center is always bad, or in serious danger. If there is a solid pawn barrier in front of it, then the king can feel secure in his fortress. But you don't encounter such exceptions very often. In most cases, an uncastled king is a juicy target.

Principles for attacking the uncastled king

The presence of the opposing king in the center does not by itself guarantee success for the attack. In order to get at the target you have to marshall your forces and find a way to break through whatever defense the enemy possesses. Your attack must be prepared, and there are two characterisics of such preparation. First, you have to have *superior development*. Second, you must grab hold of the *initiative*.

When attacking an uncastled king, you should try to:

1. Prevent the enemy king from fleeing the central area. The king is usually in much greater danger in the middle of the board.

2. Open as many lines (files and diagonals) as possible leading toward the enemy king.

3. Involve as many of your pieces in the attack as you can. The more pieces you use, the easier it is to develop an offensive, and the more difficult the defensive task becomes.

4. Keep the opposing army disorganized. When the king is in the center on the back rank, it interferes with the communication between the rooks, and this makes it more difficult to organize the defense. It is

best to keep your opponent's lines of communication broken.

Keep these four principles in mind as we look at some examples of successful attacks against the king in the center.

Sacrifice to open lines

Diagram 1
Morphy—Amateur
New Orleans 1858, blindfold simul

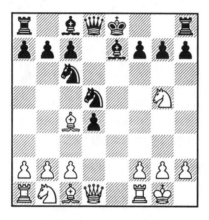

Position after Black's 7th move

By sacrificing a piece White keeps the opponent's king in the center and organizes a direct attack.

8. Nxf7!	Kxf7
9. Qf3+	

Diagram 2

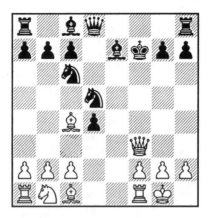

9. ...   Ke6

Black must play this move to keep the extra piece, or else White will have the advantage without any risk. Other moves don't give Black any hope for equality:

A) 9. ... Ke8 10. Bxd5 Rf8 (10. ... Ne5 11. Qh5+ Ng6 12. Re1, or 10. ... Qd6 11. Qf7+ Kd8 12. Qxg7 Bf6 13. Bg5) 11. Bxc6+ bxc6 12. Qxc6+ Bd7 13. Qc4 and Black doesn't have compensation for a pawn.

B) 9. ... Bf6 10. Bxd5+ Be6 11. Bxe6+. (Winning a pawn in this position makes no sense because after 11. Bxc6 bxc6 12. Qxc6, Black has better development and two strong bishops.) 11. ... Kxe6 and now, after the simple 12. Bf4, Black's king is uncomfortably placed in the center and cannot find refuge; for example, 12. ... Kf7 13. Qb3+, or 12. ... Kd7 13. Qh3+.

10. Nc3!

This sacrifice helps White develop his attack in a swift and forceful manner. In this game the opponent's king ended up literally in the center of the board!

Diagram 3

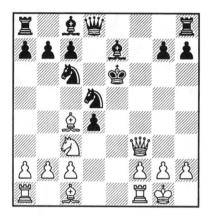

10. ...	dxc3
11. Re1+	Ne5

Black's reply is forced.

| 12. Bf4 | Bf6 |

If Black tries 12. ... c6, White plays 13. Rxe5+ Kd7 (if 13. ... Kf7 instead, there follows 14. Bxd5+ cxd5 15. Rxe7+ winning the queen or creating an irresistible attack) 14. Rxd5+ cxd5 15. Qxd5+ Ke8 16. Qf7+ Kd7 17. Bb5 mate.

| 13. Bxe5 | Bxe5 |

Diagram 4

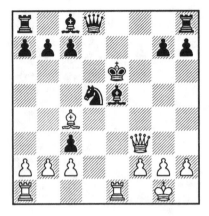

14. Rxe5+!	Kxe5
15. Re1+	Kd4
16. Bxd5	

Diagram 5

Black has an extra rook, but his "centralized" king appears to be in a mating net. Right now White's main threat is 17. Qxc3+ Kxd5 18. Re5+ Kd6 19. Qc5+ Kd7 20. Qd5 mate. In addition, White is also threatening 17. Qe4+ Kc5 18. b4+ Kb5 (If 18. ... Kb6, then 19. Qd4+ Ka6 20. Qc4+ b5 21. Qc6 mate, and 18. ... Kd6 will be followed by 19. Qe5+ Kd7 20. Qe6 mate)

19. a4+ Kxa4 20. Ra1+ with mate to follow. The same idea can be seen after 17. Qd3+ Kc5 18. b4+ etc.

Of course now Black cannot recapture with 16. ... Qxd5? because of 17. Qxc3 mate. Let's look at some other possible variations:

1) 16. ... c6 17. Qe3+ Kxd5 18. Qe5+ Kc4 19. Re4+ and mate next move.

2) 16. ... Qf6 17. Rd1+ Kc5 (or 17. ... Ke5 18. Qe4+ Kd6 19. Bc4+) 18. Qe3+ Kb5 19. a4+ Kxa4 20. Qe4+, etc.

3) 16. ... Qg5 17. Qd3+ Kc5 18. b4+ Kxb4 19. Qd4+.

4) 16. ... Qd6 17. b4 Qxb4 18. Re4+ Kc5 19. Qe3+.

16. ...	**Re8**
17. Qd3+	**Kc5**
18. b4+!	**Kxb4**
19. Qd4+	

Diagram 6

And White will announce checkmate in a few moves. In this game Morphy showed excellent technique in pursuing the attack on the king in the center. White's play is even more impressive when we consider that the game was played more than a hundred years ago in what is known as a simultaneous blindfold exhibition!

Punishment for losing time in the opening

Diagram 7
Anderssen — Kieseritsky
London, 1851

1. e4	e5
2. f4	exf4
3. Bc4	Qh4+
4. Kf1	b5

The purpose of this counter-sacrifice is to deflect White's bishop from the f7-square.

5. Bxb5	Nf6
6. Nf3	Qh6

Diagram 8

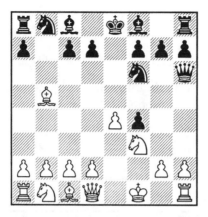

It seems more natural to play 6. ... Qh5, but Kieseritsky wants to leave the h5-square vacant for the knight. The move 6. ... Qh6 is characteristic of games from the last century, and is a good illustration of the thinking of that time. By this we mean the tendency to play for tactics alone, without sufficient attention to control of the center and the coordination of the pieces.

7. d3   Nh5

Diagram 9

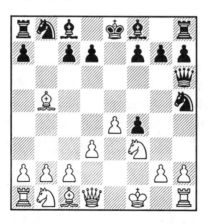

Black builds his game on small tactical threats which are easy to stop. Better was 9. ... c6.

8. Nh4

The threat was 8. ... Ng3+. On 8. Kg1? Black would play 8. ... Qb6+.

8. ...	Qg5

Also deserving attention is 8. ... Bb7, so that on 9. g4 Nf6 10. Nf5 Black has the reply 10. ... Qh3+.

9. Nf5	c6
10. g4	Nf6

Diagram 10

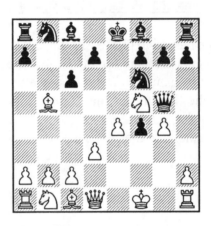

11. Rg1!

When he offered his bishop to Kieseritsky, Anderssen could not have calculated all the variations to the end. But the awkward position of Black's queen, plus White's advantage in development, make this a promising piece sacrifice. Notice that in order to accept the material, Black must also weaken his d5-square.

11. ...	cxb5
12. h4	Qg6
13. h5	Qg5
14. Qf3	

Diagram 11

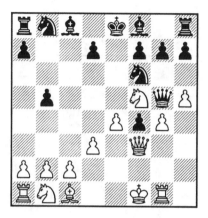

Now the threat is 15. Bxf4, trapping Black's queen. Black is forced to lose more tempi in order to provide a retreat.

14. ...   **Ng8**
15. Bxf4   **Qf6**

Diagram 12

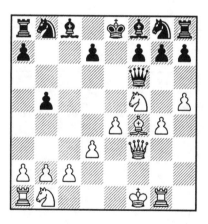

The sad outcome of the opening is a gaping hole on d5, and a huge advantage for White in the mobilization of his forces. We can see all the preconditions for a decisive attack on the king.

16. Nc3	Bc5
17. Nd5!	

Diagram 13

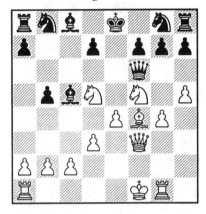

Of course there is no happiness for Black in the simple 17. d4. However, Anderssen sensed that the time was right for more energetic action.

17. ...	Qxb2

Now both of White's rooks are under attack.

Diagram 14

18. Bd6!?

This quiet move, which offers a double rook sacrifice, made a great impact on the chess world at the time this game was played. However, the superiority of White's position is without question. His queen and three minor pieces are ready to demolish Black's king, which is stuck in the center. Black's queen is out on a long journey and is unable to help the king.

No wonder that in addition to the very effective move played by Anderssen (18. Bd6), White had another, objectively stronger continuation of attack — *18. Be3.* Here are some variations:

(A) **18. ... Qxa1+** 19. Kg2 Qxg1+. (If 19. ... Qb2, then 20. Bxc5 Qxc2+ 21. Kh3 Qxc5 22. Rc1, and White will win, e.g. 22. ... Qxc1 23. Nd6+ Kd8 24. Nxf7+ Ke8 25. Nd6+ and 26. Qf8 mate.) 20. Bxg1 and Black has no defense against White's threats:

(A1) *20. ... Bxg1* 21. Nd6+ Kd8 22. Nxf7+ Ke8 23. Nd6+ and 24. Qf8 mate.

(A2) *20. ... d6* 21. Bxc5 Bxf5. (Instead 21. ... dxc5 will be followed by checkmate in seven moves with 22. Nd6+ Kd7 23. Qxf7+ Kxd6 24. Qc7+ Ke6 etc.) 22. Nc7+ Kd7 23. Nxa8 dxc5 24. Qxf5+ Kd8 25. Qe5, with an easy win.

(A3) *20. ... Bf8* 21. Nc7+ Kd8 22. Nxa8 Bb7 23. Bxa7 Nc6 24. Bb6+ Kc8 25. Qg3 and White wins.

(B) **18. ... Qa3** (18. ... Bf8 19. Bd4) 19. Bxc5 Qxc5 20. e5 d6 21. Nxd6+ Kd7 22. Qf5+ Kc6 23. Qxc8+ Kxd5 24. c4+ bxc4 25. dxc4+ Kd4 26. Rd1+, and Black gets checkmated.

(C) **18. ... d6** 19. Bd4! Bxd4 20. Nxd6+ Kd8 (20. ... Kd7 21. Qxf7+ Kxd6 22. Qc7+ Ke6 23. Nf4+ Kf6 24. g5 mate) 21. Qxf7 with unstoppable checkmate threats.

| 18. ... | Bxg1 |

Diagram 15

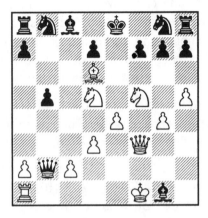

After this Anderssen's combination wins by force. But as Steinitz pointed out, 18. ... Qxa1+ 19. Ke2 Qb2! left some hope for Black. Even though Anderssen's idea is widely acknowledged as a stroke of genius, his precise method of implementing that idea can still be improved. *A combination is only beautiful when it is correct.* A sacrifice should not only be the most effective, but also *objectively* the best continuation.

19. e5!!

Diagram 16

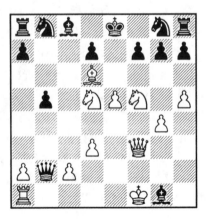

Another remarkably quiet move. Already one rook and a minor piece down, Anderssen allows his opponent to take the second rook with a check! But by blocking the a1-h8 diagonal and cutting off the Black queen from defending the g7-square, White is now threatening checkmate with 20. Nxg7+ and 21. Bc7.

19. ...	**Qxa1+**
20. Ke2	

Now Kieseritsky protects c7 to stop the mate threat: 21. Nxg7+ Kd8 22. Bc7 mate.

20. ...	**Na6**
21. Nxg7+	**Kd8**
22. Qf6+!	

The final sacrifice, deflecting the knight from the defense of e7.

22. ...	**Nxf6**
23. Be7 mate.	

Diagram 17

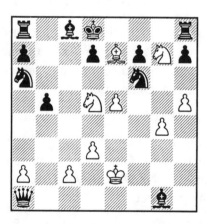

This game shows how dangerous it is to play with only one or two pieces, neglecting development. In the final position White is down a queen, two rooks and a bishop! In 1855 *Wiener Schachzeitung* magazine published a detailed analysis of this game, where for the first time it was described as "The Immortal Game."

Exchanging to prevent castling

Diagram 18
Steinitz — von Bardeleben
Hastings, 1895

Position after Black's 10th move

At first it may seem as though Black has a satisfactory position. However, with a simple series of exchanges, White keeps the Black king in the center and then creates an attack followed by an effective combination.

11. Bxd5!   **Bxd5**

It's not good to take the bishop on g5 because after 11. ... Bxg5 12. Bxe6 fxe6 13. Qb3 Black is unable to protect the e6-pawn, and on 13. ... Nxd4 there would follow 14. Nxd4 Qxd4 15. Qb5+, winning a piece.

12. Nxd5   **Qxd5**

Taking the bishop on g5 is still bad since Black loses a pawn: 12. ... Bxg5 13. Nxc7+ Qxc7 14. Nxg5.

13. Bxe7   Nxe7
14. Re1

Diagram 19

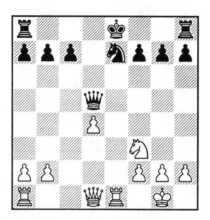

This is the point of White's previous play. By pinning the knight, White prevents Black from castling into safety, and keeps the Black king in the "danger zone" in the center of the board.

14. ...   f6

Black prepares an exit on f7 for his king, since he cannot castle.

15. Qe2   Qd7

The Black queen not only had to protect the knight, but also had to cover the b5-square.

16. Rc1

The second rook also occupies an important file.

16. ...   c6?

This overly optimistic move is probably a decisive mistake. Instead 16. ... Kf7 was more logical, to connect the rooks and eventually to bring his king to safety.

17. d5!

Diagram 20

This remarkable pawn sacrifice opens a second file and also frees the central square d4 for the knight, from where he will threaten to invade the opponent's camp, especially on the weakened e6-square. If Black declines the sacrifice, then after 18. dxc6 White will create an attack on the open central files while maintaining material equality.

17. ...	cxd5
18. Nd4	Kf7
19. Ne6	Rhc8

Black defends against a rook invasion on c7. If 19. ... Nc6, then 20. Nc5; for example, 20. ... Qc8 21. Qh5+, etc.

20. Qg4	g6

Diagram 21

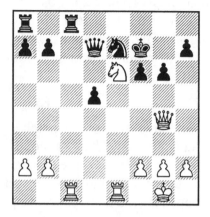

There is no other defense because 20. ... Ng6 will be followed by the winning move 21. Ng5+, and if 20. ... Rxc1 then White mates in two with 21. Qxg7+ Ke8 22. Qf8 mate.

21. Ng5+   Ke8

Now White uncorks a brilliant combination, made possible because of the unfavorable placement of Black's king in the center.

22. Rxe7+!

Diagram 22

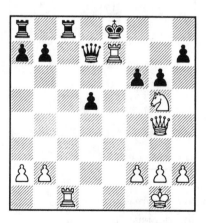

Now on 22. ... Qxe7 White wins after the simple 23. Rxc8+.
If 22. ... Kxe7 then 23. Re1+ Kd6 24. Qb4+ Kc7 (24. ... Rc5 is
met by 25. Re6+) 25. Ne6+ Kb8 26. Qf4+ Rc7 27. Nxc7, etc.
After considering all of those variations, we might come to the
conclusion that White is simply winning. However, Black can
counter with a witty reply.

22. ...   Kf8!

White does not have an escape hatch against Black's
threatened back-rank mate, so White cannot take the queen. At
the same time, all of White's pieces are under attack!
Nevertheless White's combination is correct. Steinitz saw
further than his opponent and anticipated this position.

23. Rf7+ !   Kg8!

It is bad to take the rook because of 24. Rxc8+.

24. Rg7+!   Kh8!

The reply 24. ... Kf8 loses immediately to 25. Nxh7+.

25. Rxh7+!   Kg8
26. Rg7+!   Kh8

Diagram 23

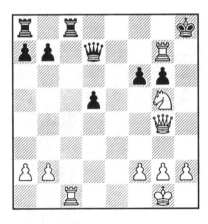

By taking the h7-pawn White opened the h-file, so that now
the queen lands the decisive blow.

27. Qh4+	Kxg7
28. Qh7+	Kf8
29. Qh8+	Ke7
30. Qg7+	Ke8
31. Qg8+	Ke7
32. Qf7+	Kd8
33. Qf8+	Qe8
34. Nf7+	Kd7
35. Qd6 mate.	

Diagram 24

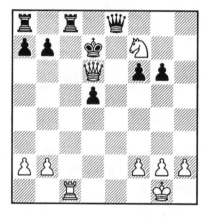

The final position makes a strong impression. Notice especially the useless Black rook on a8.

Recall the Principles for
Attacking the Uncastled King

1. Keep the opposing king in the center.

2. Open lines to the opposing king.

3. Involve as many of your pieces in the attack as you can.

4. Keep the enemy disorganized.

(See page 14 for details.)

Lack of harmony

Diagram 25
Tchigorin — Salwe
8th match game, 1906

Position after Black's 13th move

White stands better because Black has not castled and his pawn structure is poor. The best way to exploit these advantages is to open the central files.

14. Bxc6!   **bxc6**

14. ... Bxc6 could be followed by 15. Ndxf5 exf5 16. Rfe1 Rd7 (if 16. ... Qc5 then 17. b4!) 17. Rad1 Qc7 (if 17. ... Qc5 then 18. b4!) 18. Nxf5 and White wins the bishop on e7.

15. Rfe1

With the threat 16. Ndxf5.

15. ...   **Qc5**
16. Rad1   **...**

Again, the threat is 17. Ndxf5 and if 17. ... exf5 then 18. b4.

16. ...   **f4**

On 16. ... Bc8 White would win with the combination 17. Ngxf5 exf5 18. Qxe7+ Qxe7 19. Rxe7+ Kxe7 20. Nxc6+.

| 17. Ne4 | Qe5 |
| 18. Qf3 | Qc7 |

Diagram 26

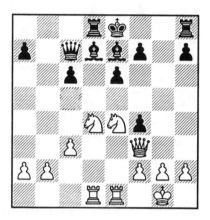

Black did not castle here because of the weakness of the pawns on f4 and c6. For example 18. ... 0-0 19. Ne2 f5 (trying to save the pawn) 20. Nd2 Bg5 21. h4 Bh6 22. Nc4 Qc5 23. b3 e5 24. Rd6 Bg7 25. Red1, etc.

| 19. Qh5 | Bc8 |

On 19. ... c5, 20. Nf5 would be very strong.

| 20. Ng5 | ... |

The threat is not only 21. Qxf7+ but also 21. Ngxe6.

| 20. ... | Bxg5 |
| 21. Qxg5 | h5 |

Diagram 27

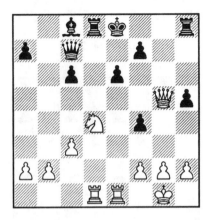

22. Nf5!

White is not satisfied with winning a pawn after 22. Nxc6, and continues the attack instead, threatening 23. Ng7+.

22. ...	Rd5
23. c4!	Rxd1
24. Rxd1	exf5

Diagram 28

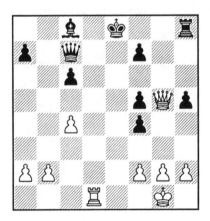

Black has to accept the knight sacrifice because there is no other defense to 25. Ng7+.

25. Qg7	Rf8
26. Re1+	Be6
27. Rxe6+!	

Diagram 29

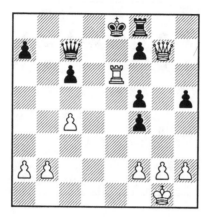

Even though the position has been simplified, White's attack continues because of the bad position of Black's king. Besides that, Black has six (!) isolated pawns.

27. ...	Kd7
28. Rh6	Qa5

On 28. ... Re8 White could have traded into a winning king and pawn ending with 29. Qxf7+ Kd8 30. Qxe8+, etc.

29. Qd4+	Ke8
30. h3	f6
31. Qxf4	Kd7
32. Rxh5	Qxa2
33. Rh7+	Black resigns.

A practical decision

Diagram 30
Gruenfeld — Spielmann
Shopron, 1934

Position after White's 12th move

The Black pieces are perfectly developed, but if Black doesn't act quickly his temporary advantage in development will evaporate. Since the White king is still in the center of the board, Black should of course think about attacking him. But how can he do it?

This position currently has a closed character. Both of Black's bishops are limited in their activities. The open c-file cannot be used efficiently, and it is the only open file on the board. After initially considering this position, we can speculate that Black's advantage in development does not give him real chances to assume the initiative, and that White will be able to equalize by finishing his development.

GM Spielmann, however, was a brilliant tactician, and he finds an interesting way of developing the initiative.

12. ...   e5!

A completely unexpected and beautiful move, the meaning of which will become clear in a moment.

13. fxe5

White is forced to take the pawn, because otherwise the center will become open and his lack of development will become more important.

13. ...   Nxe5!

Black's whole idea is in this sacrifice. Again, White has no choice since after 14. Be2 Nc4! Black assumes the initiative at no cost.

14. dxe5

Diagram 31

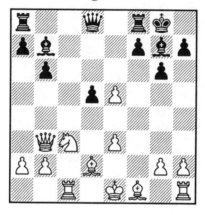

14. ...   d4!

Now Black is very close to his goal of opening up the game. The question is whether or not the newly opened lines of attack are worth the piece sacrifice. It is interesting that Spielmann in his book *The Art of Sacrifice in Chess* said of this position:

> The opening-up of lines must be carried out ruthlessly. In annotating this game for a chess periodical, I wrote the following comment at this stage: *The sacrifice of the knight cannot be vindicated by analysis, and it would possibly have been refuted in a correspondence game. But in a contest over the board and with a time limit of eighteen moves an hour, it would nearly always win out.*

From this we can conclude that Spielmann himself was not sure whether or not the sacrifice was correct, when approaching the question from a theoretical point of view. Should this confuse us?

No, it should not. We gave this example to you on purpose, because we consider it a useful reminder that unclear sacrifices like this one — which do not immediately lead to mate or the win of material — are very common.

Diagram 32

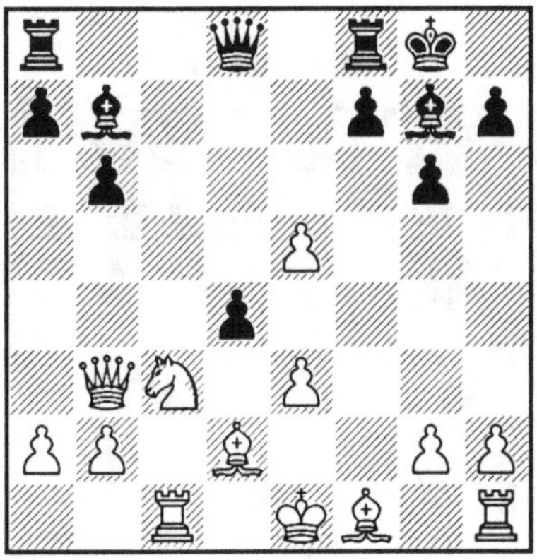

15. Nd1

After 15. Ne2 Bxe5 16. exd4 Bxd4 17. Nxd4 Qxd4, Black has only one pawn for the piece, but the White king will remain in the center for quite a while, and Black should be able to use all his pieces in an attack.

Deserving attention is 15. exd4. In that case it would be better for Black to decline the check on h4 and play simply 15. ... Qxd4, because 15. ... Qh4+ 16. Kd1 Qxd4 would let White bring his king to a comparatively safe place: 17. Qa4 (if 17. Kc2, then 17. ... Rac8) 17. ... Qxe5 18. Kc2.

15. ...	Bxe5
16. e4	

Diagram 33

White is defending in an original manner by giving away a central pawn for the purpose of closing the d-file and limiting the role of Black's dark-squared bishop, which will be blocked by its own pawn.

16. ...	Bxe4
17. Nf2	Bd5
18. Qh3	

Diagram 34

Defending the pawn on g2. White wants to play Bd3 and then castle, after which he will have an advantage thanks to the extra piece. This plan could become a reality, for example, after 18. ... Bxa2 19. Bd3 Be6 20. Qh6 Bg7 21. Qf4, and Black's three pawns do not fully compensate for the piece because the White king is no longer in danger.

> **18. ...   Qe7**
> **19. Be2**

White's desire to castle as soon as possible is completely understandable. However, Black's next move shows that this wish will not come true, and White therefore appears to be under a serious attack.

It would also not be good to play 19. Bd3 because of 19. ... Bf4+ 20. Kd1 Bxd2 21. Kxd2 Qb4+, for example: 22. Kc2 Qa4+ 23. Kd2 Qxa2, and Black has three pawns for the piece plus an attack. Spielmann thought that the best defense would be 19. Kd1, to continue after 19. ... Bxa2 with 20. Bc4.

> **19. ...   d3!**

This sacrifice opens the game even more.

Diagram 35

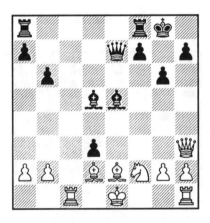

20. Nxd3

If 20. Qxd3, then Black plays 20. ... Bxg2 21. Rg1 Bb7, when his rooks will threaten the White king on the open central files.

20. ...   **Rfe8**
21. Kf1

Limits the role of the rook on h1. But after 21. Kd1, Black would win the Exchange and a pawn by 21. ... Bxb2. Also bad is 21. 0-0 Bd4+.

21. ...   **Bxb2!**

It would be wrong to play 21. ... Bc3, because after 22. Bxc3 Qxe2+ 23. Kg1 Re3 White will have the answer 24. Nf4!. When the win seems to be near, be especially alert for possible counterplay from your opponent!

Diagram 36

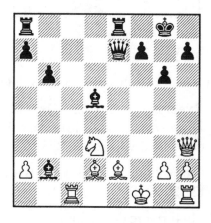

22. Re1   **Qf6+**
23. Nf2

If 23. Bf4 then 23. ... Re4 and White is completely tied up— for example, 24. Bf3 Rxe1+ 25. Kxe1 Qc3+ 26. Ke2 Re8+ 27. Be3 Qc2+, or 24. Bd1 Rxe1+ 25. Kxe1 Re8+ 26. Kf1 Bc4, etc. Other answers for White are even worse.

23. ...   **Bd4**
24. Qg3

Hopeless for White would be 24. Bf3 Bc4+ 25. Kg1 Rxe1+ 26. Bxe1 Re8.

24. ...   **Re4!**

Diagram 37

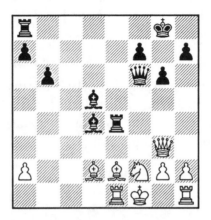

25. h4

Let's look at other possible answers for White:

a) 25. Qf3 Rxe2! 26. Qxe2 (if 26. Qxf6 Black has the in-between move 26. ... Rxe1+) and Black wins through deflection with 26. ... Bc4.

b) 25. Bf3 Bc4+ 26. Kg1 Rxe1+ 27. Bxe1 Re8 28. Bd2 Bxf2+ 29. Qxf2 Qa1+.

c) 25. Bd3 Rg4! (more deflection).

d) 25. Rc1! is the best move. Now Black does not have anything forced, but after 25. ... Re5 his attack should still eventually succeed, mainly because White's rook on h1 is shut out of the game and will remain so for a long time.

25. ...   **Rae8**

Diagram 38

26. Bb5

The threat was 26. ... Rxe2 followed by 27. ... Bc4.

26. ...   **Rxe1+**
27. Bxe1   **Re3!**

Diagram 39

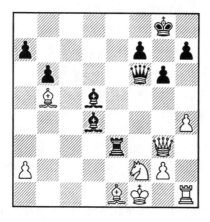

Black won quickly after **28. Qg5 Rxe1+ 29. Kxe1 Qxf2+ 30. Kd1 Bxg2 31. Re1 Bf3+ 32. Be2 Bc3 33. Bxf3 Qxf3+ 34. Kc2 Bxe1 and White resigns**.

Opening or middlegame?

Diagram 40
Tolush — Botvinnik
XI th USSR Championship, 1939

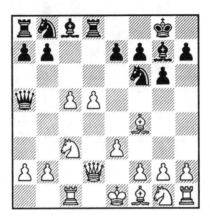

Position after White's 9th move

Black is going into the middlegame, but White seems to be stuck in the opening since he is a long way from completing the development of his pieces. To take appropriate action, Black must first take stock of the situation.

First, White's king is in the center. Second, all of White's pieces on the kingside are standing in their initial positions. Finally, Black's queen, rook, bishop and knight are placed well and — very importantly — they are interacting harmoniously. The fact that at the moment White has two extra pawns does not seem important, because one of them can be taken immediately and the other would hardly be enough compensation for the weaknesses in White's position.

Let's see how the fight went, and analyze the main variations.

9. ...   Nxd5

Diagram 41

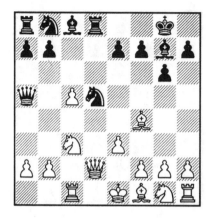

Black has such powerful threats that taking the knight on d5 seems to be the only move for White, because 10. Rd1 Bxc3 11. bxc3 Nc6, with the threats 12. ... Nxf4 and 12. ... Nxc3, favors Black. But after 10. Nxd5 Qxd2+ 11. Kxd2 Rxd5+ Black's advantage is also clear. For example: 12. Ke1 Bxb2 13. Rc2 (or 13. Bc4 Bxc1 14. Bxd5 Ba3) 13. ... Ba3 or 12. Kc2 Bf5+ 13. Kb3 Rd2, etc.

So our first impression appears to be correct: White's position is worse. However, this conclusion would be hasty, because we did not consider the move which was played in the game.

10. Bc7!?

An unexpected and beautiful move. Does it save White?

10. ...   **Qxc7**
11. Nxd5

Diagram 42

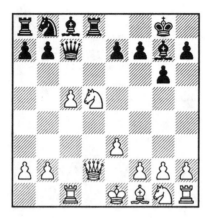

It seems that the situation has changed. If Black now plays 11. ... Qd7 White has the strong answer 12. Rd1! with the main threat 13. Nc7!, so that Black cannot respond with either 12. ... e6 or 12. ... Kf8. But instead Black has the simple developing move 12. ... Nc6 defending against this threat. How can we evaluate this position?

While we may not be able to find much noticeable improvement in the placement of White's forces, Black's position became less harmonious — the queen on d7 is not well placed because it blocks the bishop. We should conclude that after 11. ... Qd7 Black does not have sufficient compensation for his pawn minus.

However, Black has a strong reply that underlines the basic weakness in White's position (lack of development), and supports the assessment that in the initial position White stands worse.

11. ...   Rxd5!

Diagram 43

By sacrificing the Exchange, Black not only liquidates White's main trump—his centralized knight—but also finishes developing the rest of his pieces with a gain of time. It is clear that White's defense will be difficult because his whole kingside is unmoved.

12. Qxd5   Be6

Black's main goal is complete mobilization of his forces. That is why capturing the pawn on b2 would be incorrect. On 12. ... Bxb2 White would reply 13. Rc2 Qa5+ (or 13. ... Be6) 14. Qd2, winning a tempo for developing the kingside.

13. Qd2

On 13. Qe4 Black would take the pawn with 13. ... Bxb2, when it would not be possible to play 14. Rc2 because of 14. ... Bf5. And on 14. Rd1, Black plays 14. ... Qa5+.

13. ...   Nc6

Diagram 44

14. Rd1

White is facing a difficult problem — he cannot meet Black's intended ... Rd8 without serious material losses.

White's last move does nothing to develop the kingside and fails to provide a satisfactory defense. Maybe White should have tried giving back the material with 14. Rc3, after which 14. ... Rd8 is not dangerous anymore because of the answer 15. Rd3. After 14. Rc3 Bxc3 15. Qxc3 Bxa2 16. Nf3 White, too, can hope for a successful defense.

However, after 14. Rc3, Black need not be in a hurry to regain the Exchange, and should play 14. ... Nb4 (as recommended by former World Champion Botvinnik) with the better game.

14. ...	Rd8
15. Qc1	Qa5+

Diagram 45

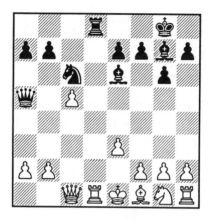

16. Rd2

The awkward 16. Ke2 is met by 16. ... Qb5+ 17. Ke1 (on 17. Kf3 Black's answer would be 17. ... Rxd1 18. Qxd1 Qxb2. After winning the a-pawn, Black will have achieved approximate material equality, while enjoying a strong passed pawn and a continuing attack.) 17. ... Rxd1+ 18. Qxd1 Qxb2 with a strong attack, which should win quickly.

Diagram 46

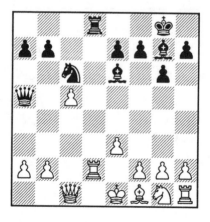

| 16. ... | Rd5 |

Black concentrates on improving the position of his pieces to the maximum. His active pieces will force White to return the invested material, with interest.

17. Ne2

After 17. Nf3 Black wins with 17. ... Rxc5—for example, 18. Qa1 Nb4 19. Nd4 Nc2+ 20. Nxc2 Rxc2 21. Qd1 Rxb2 or 18. Qb1 Bxa2 19. Qa1 Nb4, etc.

| 17. ... | Rxc5 |
| 18. Nc3 | |

Diagram 47

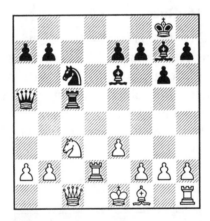

| 18. ... | Bxc3 |

This is much stronger than 18. ... Rxc3 19. bxc3 Bxc3 20. Bd3.

| 19. bxc3 | Rxc3 |
| 20. Qb2 | |

Diagram 48

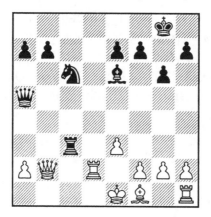

| 20. ... | Ra3 |

By maintaining the pin on the d2-rook, Black not only wins the last queenside pawn, but also continues his attack.

| 21. Qb5 | Qc3 |
| 22. Qb2 | Qc5 |

White has no defense against 23. ... Rxa2.

Diagram 49

23. Qb1

The alternative 23. Qxb7 would be followed by 23. ... Qc1+ 24. Ke2 (if 24. Rd1, then 24. ... Qc3+, and on 25. Rd2 Black will answer 25. ... Rxa2, while 25. Ke2 leads to checkmate after 25. ... Bg4+) 24. ... Bc4+ 25. Kf3 Qxd2 26. Bxc4 (White cannot take the knight in view of 26. ... Bd5+) 26. ... Ne5+ 27. Ke4 (not 27. Kg3 Rxe3+!) 27. ... Qc2+ 28. Kxe5 Qxc4, and White's king is trapped in a mating net—for example, 29. Qd5 Ra5! 30. Qxa5 f6 mate.

23. ...	**Bxa2!**
24. Rxa2	

This leads to new material losses, but other moves are also hopeless for White.

24. ...	**Qa5+**
25. Rd2	**Ra1**
26. Bd3	**Rxb1+**
27. Bxb1	

Black has a decisive advantage — his connected passed a- and b-pawns should win. We provide the rest of the game without comments. **27. ... Ne5 28. Ke2 Qb5+ 29. Bd3 Nxd3 30. Rxd3 a5 31. Rd1 Qc4 32. Kf3 b5 33. Rd7 b4 34. Ra7 a4 35. Rd8+ Kg7 36. Rda8 a3 37. g3 Qb5 White resigns.**

Unexpected sacrifice
Diagram 50
Holmov — Keres
XXVIth USSR Championship, 1959

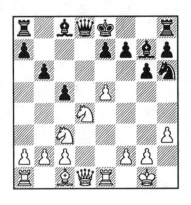

Position after Black's 11th move

White's knight is under attack, and it seems that after the horseman moves Black will have good play. However, a deep examination of the position led GM Holmov to play an unexpected move to keep Black's king in the center.

12. Nc6!

This penetration of the White knight into the enemy camp, from where there is no escape, demanded long and exact calculations.

Diagram 51

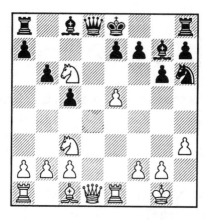

12. ...   Qd7

An important alternative is 12. ... Qxd1. After 13. Rxd1 White threatens checkmate, so Black must move the c8-bishop. After 13. ... Bb7 White plays 14. Nd5. (The paradoxical reply 14. ... Kd7 is refuted by 15. Ncxe7 followed by 16. Bg5. If 14. ... Kf8, then 15. Nc7 and 15. ... Bxc6 leads to the main variation, and 15. ... Rc8 16. Nxa7 gives White an extra pawn with an excellent position.) If, for example, 14 ... Bxc6 15. Nc7+ Kf8 16. Nxa8, and it is impossible to take the knight because of the checkmate. The same variations would occur after 13. ... Bd7 14. Nd5. White also would have an advantage after 13. ... Be6 14. Nb5 or 13. ... Bf5 14. Nd5. And on 12. ... Qc7 White plays the same move as in the game.

13. Nxe7!

Diagram 52

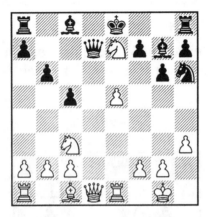

The goal of this sacrifice is to keep Black's king in the center.

13. ...   Kxe7

Let's consider Black's alternatives, 13. ... Qxe7 and 13. ... Qxd1:

1) 13. ... Qxe7 14. Nd5 Qd8 (if 14. ... Qb7, then 15. Nf6+ Bxf6 16. exf6+ Be6 17. Bxh6) 15. Nf6+ Bxf6 (or 15. ... Ke7 16. Qf3 Be6 17. Bg5 with decisive threats) 16. exf6+ Be6 17. Bxh6 Qxf6 (the ending arising after 17. ... Qxd1 18. Raxd1 would be hopeless) 18. Qg4.

Diagram 53
Analysis Diagram

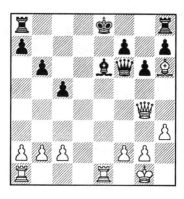

Position after 18. Qg4

Black is in trouble—18. ... Qxb2 is bad because 19. Rxe6+ fxe6 20. Qxe6+ Kd8 21. Rd1+. If 18. ... Qd4 then 19. Re4, and 18. ... 0-0-0 could be followed by 19. Bg5 Qxb2 20. Qa4! and White should win—for example, 20. ... Rd7 21. Qc6+ Rc7 22. Qa8+ Kd7 23. Rad1+, or 20. ... Rd6 21. Rad1 Rxd1 22. Qc6+.

2) From Diagram 52, 13. ... Qxd1 14. Rxd1 Kxe7 (otherwise Black will end up a pawn down in a worse position).

Diagram 54
Analysis Diagram

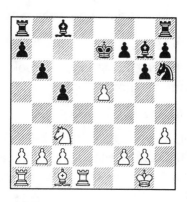

Position after 14. ... Kxe7

15. Bg5+! Ke6 16. Rd6+ Kf5 (16. ... Kxe5 17. Rd5+ Ke6
18. Re1+ leads to checkmate) 17. f4 with the main threat 18.
Bxh6 Bxh6 19. Rf6 mate, and the secondary threat 18. Ne2.
Black does not have a satisfactory defense—for example,
17. ... Be6 18. Ne2 Ke4 19. Ng3+ Ke3 and White can give
checkmate in three ways.

Now let's return to the actual game.

14. Bxh6

Diagram 55

14. ...   Bxh6

On 14. ... Qxd1 there is the in-between move 15. Bg5+.

15. Qf3   Bg7

White not only threatened to take the rook on a8 but also to
play 16. Qf6+, winning another rook.

16. Nd5+

This is stronger than 16. Qxa8 Bb7 17. Qxa7 Qc6 18. f3 Ra8
19. Nd5+ Qxd5 20. Qxb6, even though in this case White should
win thanks to his material advantage and better position.

16. ...   Kd8

If 16. ... Kf8 White beautifully finishes the game with 17. e6 Qb7 18. e7+ Ke8 19. Qf6!

17. Rad1

Diagram 56

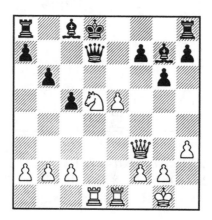

17. ...   **Bb7**

Even after the stronger 17. ... Qb7 White would win by continuing 18. e6!—for example:

1) 18. ... Bxe6 19. Rxe6 fxe6 20. Nxb6+ Kc7 21. Rd7+;

2) 18. ... fxe6 19. Nb4+! Kc7 (19. ... Ke8 20. Rxe6+; 19. ... Ke7 20. Nc6+ Ke8 21. Rd8 mate) 20. Qg3+ e5 21. Rxe5 Bd7 22. Re8+!.

18. Qb3

Now Black loses his queen.

18. ...	**Bc6**
19. Nxb6	**axb6**
20. Qxf7	

Diagram 57

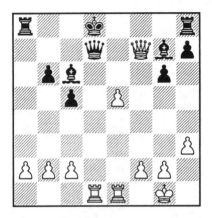

20. ... Bxe5 21. Rxd7+ Bxd7 22. Rxe5 Kc7 23. Re7 Rad8
24. a4 g5 25. Qd5 Rhe8 26. Rxh7 g4 27. a5 gxh3
28. axb6+ Kxb6 29. Rxd7 Black resigns.

Nowhere to hide

Diagram 58
Fischer — Rubinetti
Palma de Mallorca, 1970

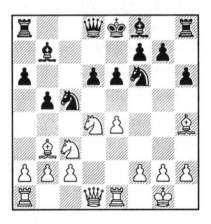

Position after Black's 11th move

12. Bd5!

A stock sacrifice in the Sicilian Defense. White opens the e-file so that his pieces can reach Black's king.

12. ...   **exd5**

If 12. ... Be7, then 13. Bxb7 Nxb7 14. Nc6 Qc7 15. Nxe7 Qxe7 16. Nd5! and now if 16. ... exd5 17. exd5, Black loses his queen; or 16. ... Qd8 17. Nxf6+ gxf6 18. Qf3, and Black cannot protect the f6-pawn.

13. exd5+   **Kd7**

Black must try to move his king away from the danger zone in the center and toward the queenside. So White now shifts play to that side of the board.

Diagram 59

14. b4   **Na4**
15. Nxa4   **bxa4**

Diagram 60

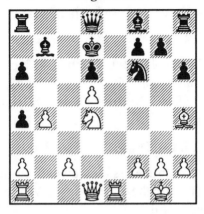

16. c4   Kc8

White calmly mobilizes his forces, secure in the knowledge that the Black king will be awkwardly placed for many moves to come. After 16. ... Rc8 17. Qxa4+ Kc7 18. Nc6 Bxc6 19. Qxc6+ Kb8 20. Qxa6, for example, White has the advantage.

17. Qxa4   Qd7
18. Qb3

Diagram 61

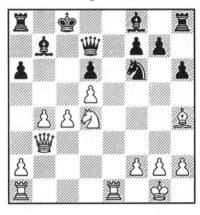

18. ...   g5

Both this move and Black's next one make White's task of advancing the c-pawn easier to accomplish. Better would have been 18. ... Be7 so that the rook on h8 could enter the battle and perform some defensive functions. The bishop would provide additional support and there would then be some hope of exchanging pieces and blunting the attack. When trying to defend after a sacrifice, rapid development is essential.

But even here Black would not have survived long because he is too far behind in development and has too many problems to solve. Let's look at a sample line: 18. ... Be7 19. Rac1 Re8 20. Red1! and White is effectively playing with an extra rook: 20. ... Ne4 (or 20. ... a5 21. Bxf6! gxf6 22. c5 dxc5 23. d6 Qxd6 24. bxc5 Qd5 25. Qh3+ Qd7 26. Nf5! and Black is overwhelmed) 21. Bxe7 Rxe7 22. c5 dxc5 23. d6!.

19. Bg3	Nh5

Diagram 62

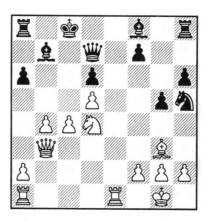

20. c5	dxc5
21. bxc5	Qxd5

No better is 21. ... Bxd5 22. Qb6 Nxg3 23. c6 Bxc6 24. Rac1.

22. Re8+	Kd7

Diagram 63

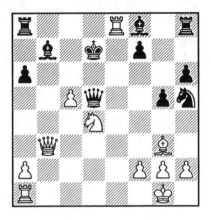

23. Qa4+	Bc6
24. Nxc6	

Diagram 64

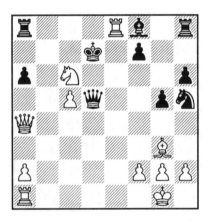

Black resigns, because on 24. ... Kxe8 White plays 25. Re1+, and 24. ... Qxc6 runs into 25. Rd1+.

Probing for weaknesses

Diagram 65
Fischer — Dely
Skopje, 1967

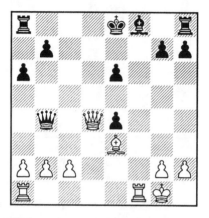

Position after Black's 15th move

The future World Champion has energetically conducted the attack against his opponent's uncastled king. Now he finishes with a flourish.

16. Rxf8+!   Qxf8
17. Qa4+!

Diagram 66

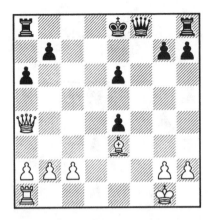

17. ...   b5

White has noticed the Black king is boxed in by two open files, and so he forces Black to open even more lines. Moving the king would be worse: 17. ... Ke7 is met by 18. Bc5+; 17. ... Kf7 fails to 18. Rf1+; and 17. ... Kd8 fails to 18. Bb6+ Kc8 19. Qc4+ Kd7 20. Rd1+ Ke8 21. Qa4+.

18. Qxe4

Diagram 67

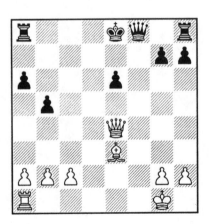

Now it's clear that the point of 17. Qa4+ was to open the long
diagonal h1-a8 for White's queen.

18. ...   Rd8

Other moves also lose: 18. ... Kd7 19. Qb7+ Kd6 20. Rd1+
Ke5 21. Bd4+; 18. ... Rb8 19. Qc6+ Kd8 20. Bg5+; or 18. ... Rc8
19. Qxe6+ Kd8 20. Rd1+ Kc7 21. Qb6 mate.

19. Qc6+	**Rd7**
20. Rd1	**Qe7**
21. Bb6	

Diagram 68

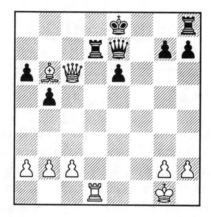

There is no defense to 22. Qc8+, so **Black resigns**.

Pursuit

Diagram 69
Tatai — Karpov
Las Palmas, 1977

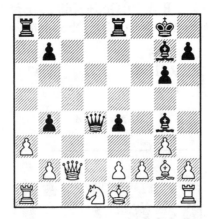

Position after White's 23rd move

In this position, Black is down a pawn but all of his forces are well developed, while White has difficulty completing his mobilization because of the poorly placed knight at d1. White's main problem is that he hasn't found time to castle. Given enough time, White will correct these problems, so Black looks for a radical way to keep White's king in the center.

23. ...   Qd3!!

Diagram 70

24. exd3

There is no good way to decline the sacrifice. If 24. Qxd3 exd3 25. e3, Black plays 25. ... d2+! 26. Kxd2 Red8+ 27. Ke1 (27. Kc2 Rac8+ 28. Kb3 bxa3) 27. ... bxa3 28. f3 axb2 29. Rb1 Be6 30. Nxb2 Ba2, winning material.

24. ...   exd3+

This discovered check and the pursuit of White's king that follows is Black's main idea.

Diagram 71

25. Kd2	Re2+
26. Kxd3	

Diagram 72

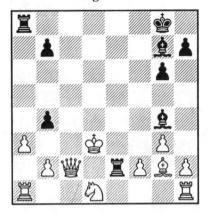

26. ...	Rd8+
27. Kc4	Rxc2+
28. Kxb4	Rcd2
29. f3	Bf8+
30. Ka5	Bd7

Diagram 73

White resigns. The main threat is 31. ... Rxg2, but Black also has 31. ... Bc5, threatening 32. ... Ra8 mate.

Suicide

Diagram 74
Anand — Kasparov
13th match game, New York, 1996

Position after Black's 11th move

12. Nxc6?!

A dubious innovation that helps Black strengthen his center.

12. ...	bxc6
13. Bh6	c5
14. Bc4?!	

Preferable is 14. Bxg7 Kxg7 15. Qe2, although Black has a good position here too.

Diagram 75

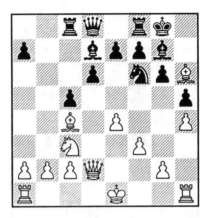

14. ...	Qb6
15. Bxg7	Kxg7
16. b3	

An artificial solution. White should have played 16. O-O-O to get his king out of the center.

Diagram 76

16. ...	Be6!

A strong reply. After 17. Bxe6 fxe6 18. O-O-O c4, Black has a powerful attack.

Diagram 77

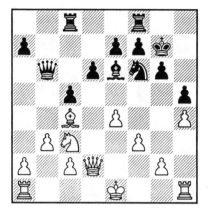

17. Nd5	Bxd5
18. exd5	e5!

Diagram 78

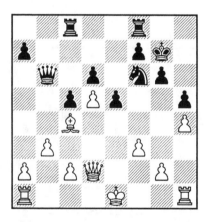

White's plan had been to pressure Black's backward e7-pawn, but now this is clearly impossible.

19. dxe6 e.p.?

With this mistake, White opens lines against his own king. Again correct is 19. O-O-O (or even 19. O-O) with only a small advantage for Black.

Diagram 79

19. ...   **d5!**

Now 20. Bxd5? loses to 20. ... Rfd8 21. c4 fxe6.

20. Be2

Diagram 80

20. ...   **c4!**

An excellent move that further delays White from castling.

21. c3?

White could still probably hold after 21. Rd1, intending Qd4 followed by Kf2 or O-O.

21. ...	Rce8
22. bxc4	

After 22. exf7 Rxf7 Black will continue with ... Rfe7 with a big advantage, and 22. Qd4 Qxe6 is also strong for Black.

22. ...	Rxe6
23. Kf1	

Or 23. cxd5 Re5 24. Kf1 Nxd5.

Diagram 81

23. ...	Rfe8
24. Bd3	dxc4
25. Bxc4	

Diagram 82

25. ...   Ne4!
White resigns.

Diagram 83

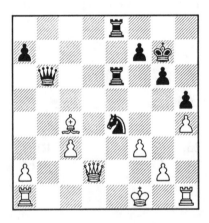

If 26.Qe1 then 26. ... Rd6 with decisive advantage for Black; 26. fxe4 loses to 26. ... Rf6+ 27. Ke1 Rxe4+ 28. Be2 Qf2+ 29. Kd1 Rxe2 30. Qxe2 Rd6+; and after 26. Qd4+ Qxd4 27. cxd4 Nd2+ wins the bishop.

Lesson Two

When the King is Safe in the Center

In Lesson One we saw many examples of why it is dangerous to leave the king uncastled. But we also said that it's not *always* bad for the king to stay in the center. Castling may not be necessary (or may not even be desirable!) when the center of the board is blocked by pawns.

Let's look at some positions in which one side's king is well placed in the center.

Is castling necessary?

Diagram 84
Kmoch — Alekhine
Vienna, 1922

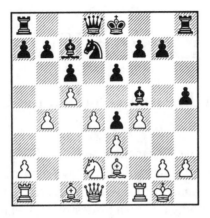

Position after White's 12th move

Both sides are approximately equally developed. Black's king is still in the center, and if this were always a serious disadvantage, then of course Black should think about castling. It is bad for Black to castle short now because the h5-pawn is under attack. And playing ... Qe7 with the idea of castling long is dangerous because White is well placed for a pawn advance on that wing.

By rigidly thinking that castling is always necessary, in this position we would be making a mistake. Why should we be in a hurry to castle? In the center Black has a strong wall of pawns, which prevents the possibility of actually opening the game. *And since this position is closed*, Black's king is probably safe on his home square.

Of course, without castling it will be difficult for Black to use his rook on a8 for activities on the kingside. But notice that the White rook on a1 also will not play an active role if Black develops an attack on the other side of the board. When the center is locked, play then shifts to the wings. Ironically, it is White who stands worse here, because *he has castled!*

By thinking along these lines, we come to the conclusion that Black can start active play on the kingside without worrying about removing his king from the center.

12. ...   g5!

Black is not worried about 13. Bxh5 because then 13. ... gxf4 14. exf4 will be followed by 14. ... Qh4 with a winning attack. Also 13. fxg5 simply opens the g-file for the attack. In his notes to this game, Alekhine wrote that best for White is 13. Nc4. But even in this case, after the simple 13. ... gxf4 14. exf4 Nf6, Black stands better, with play on the open g-file and chances against White's weak d-pawn.

13. g3

White made this move so that 13. ... gxf4 could be met by 14. gxf4. However, this move also weakens the squares around White's king.

Diagram 85

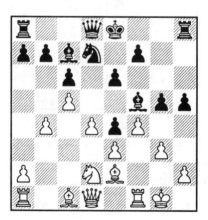

13. ...   Nf6!

If 13. ... h4, then White would prevent the opening of files by 14. g4. Here 14. fxg5 is bad because of 14. ... Ng4.

14. Bb2

It would be better to play 14. Nc4, because now Black immediately opens the position of the king.

14. ...	**gxf4**
15. exf4	

On 15. gxf4 Black would play 15. ... Nd5, forking two pawns.

15. ...	**h4**
16. Qb3	

After 16. g4 Rg8 17. h3 Nd5, White would lose the pawn on f4.

16. ...	**hxg3**
17. hxg3	**Nd5**

Diagram 86

With the opening of the h-file, we can see that White has no defense against the threat of sacrificing the piece on f4 and then moving the queen to h4.

18. Nc4	**Nxf4!**

White is lost.

19. Rae1	**Qg5**
20. d5	**Nd3!**
White resigns.	

Harmonious regrouping

Diagram 87
Kotov — Keres
Budapest, 1950

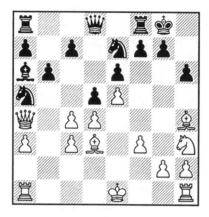

Position after Black's 13th move

How would you assess the position in the diagram above? Black's pieces are fully mobilized, and his last move (... d7-d5) attacks, and threatens to win, White's weak c4-pawn. The White king is still in the center, and his queen and knight are not well placed. Even worse, White cannot protect the c4-pawn, so it seems that to save it White must exchange his strong e5-pawn with e5xd6 *en passant*. This sort of reasoning leads to the conclusion that Black's position is better, but this conclusion would be wrong.

For if we look more deeply into the position, we can see that it is impossible for Black to threaten the White king, which is very safe behind the strong wall of pawns. In fact, it is the position of Black's king that has been weakened (by ... h7-h6). White can coordinate his pieces toward the enemy kingside. Both of White's bishops are already pointed in that direction. White's task is to find a way to bring his queen and knight into the attack. Notice also that two of Black's minor pieces are far away from the king's flank, and the third one is pinned at the moment. Kotov's next move is therefore quite logical, and gives him a strong attack on the Black king.

14. Bb1!

White abandons his pawn on c4! It is rare to see this kind of move followed by an exclamation mark, but in this particular situation this move is the strongest. White plans to play Qc2, threatening mate. What can Black do? If 14. ... Bxc4 then 15. Qc2 g6 16. Qd2 Kh7 17. Bf6 Nb3 18. Ng5+ hxg5 19. Qxg5 or 18. ... Kg8 19. Qf4 Nxa1 20. Qh4 h5 21. Qxh5! gxh5 22. Bh7 mate. If 14. ... f6, then 15. Nf4. Unpinning the e7-knight with 14. ... Qe8 is not good either, e.g. 15. Qc2 Ng6 (if 15. ... Nf5 then 16. g4) 16. cxd5 exd5 17. Nf4.

14. ...   g5

Black unpins his knight with the idea of using it for defense, but Kotov effectively refutes this maneuver.

15. Qc2   Ng6

After 15. ... Nf5 the knight is too exposed, either by the immediate 16. g4, or 16. Bf2 with the threat of g2-g4.

Diagram 88

16. Nf4!

Let us go back to the initial position (Diagram 87). Could we imagine that after just three moves all of White's minor pieces and queen would interact as well as they do now?

| 16. ... | gxh4 |

Other moves are equally unsatisfactory. For example: 16. ... Qe8 17. Nh5 Qc6 (if 17. ... f5 then 18. exf6 e.p. gxh4 19. cxd5 exd5+ 20. Kf2 or 19. ... Kh7 20. Kf2 and White's rook will come into play on the e-file) 18. cxd5 exd5 19. Bg3 and White's attack, after the break on h4 or f4, will be very strong.

| 17. Nxg6 | Re8 |
| 18. Nh8! | |

Just the type of move many players would miss! White clears a path for his queen.

18. ...	Re7
19. Qh7+	Kf8
20. f4	

Diagram 89

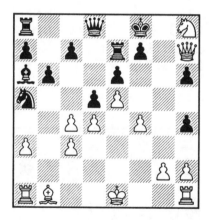

White is preparing f4-f5 in order to bring his rook into the attack on the f-file. Black's king cannot escape through e8 because after 20. ... Ke8 21. Nxf7 Rxf7 22. Bg6 Qe7 23. f5, Black is helpless.

20. ...	Nxc4
21. f5!	exf5
22. 0-0	

Diagram 90

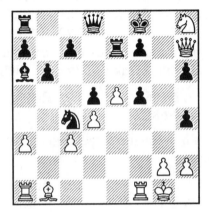

White has achieved his goal. The rook on f1 now menaces the enemy king.

22. ...	Bc8
23. Bxf5	Bxf5
24. Rxf5	Ke8
25. Rxf7	

Diagram 91

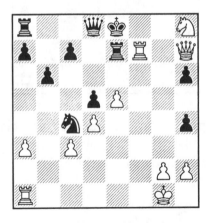

| 25. ... | Kd7 |

Black doesn't even have any extra material to compensate him for his bad position.

26. Qf5+	Kc6
27. Qf6+	Kd7
28. e6+	Kc6

Or 28. ... Kd6 29. Rxe7 Qxe7 30. Nf7+.

| 29. Rxe7 | Qxh8 |

Diagram 92

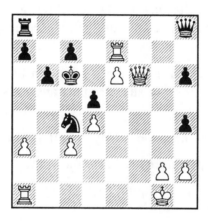

30. Rxc7+!

A final shot!

| 30. ... | Kb5 |

The alternative is 30. ... Kxc7 31. Qe7+ Kc8 (if 31. ... Kc6, then 32. Qd7 mate) 32. Rf1.

31. Qe7	a5
32. Qd7+	Ka6
33. Rab1	**Black resigns.**

Correctly evaluating the king in the center

The last two examples (of Part I) should help you in determining how to evaluate the position correctly. Most of the time it is ill-advised to leave the king in the center because it is usually possible for the other side to open the game and develop an attack on the uncastled king. However, it's important not to overestimate the negative side of this situation. *If the position is of a closed character, then having the king in the center may sometimes even be desirable.*

The player who wants to improve his level of play must learn to weigh the advantages and disadvantages of castling, and to draw correct conclusions about whether it is good or bad for the king to remain in the center through the opening and into the middlegame.

In all cases where having one's king in the center may be considered an error, the attacker must answer some important questions:

1. How do I keep the enemy king in the center?

2. Can I open more lines near the king?

3. Are my threats strong enough to give me the initiative?

4. How will I break into my opponent's position?

Solving these problems may require the sacrifice of material (sometimes in ways that are impossible to calculate completely), and may involve taking some risks. Not every player is willing to accept the same level of risk-taking, even when it is based on something very specific (such as the king trapped in the center). Insecurity about taking risks arises from a lack of knowledge and experience. Confidence in evaluating positions grows as the result of training and practice.

Exercises

1

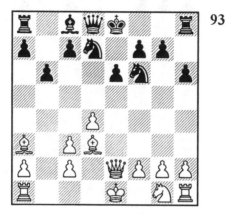

93

White to move

2

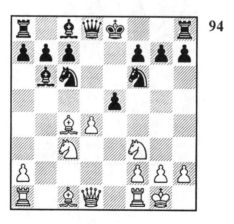

94

White to move

3

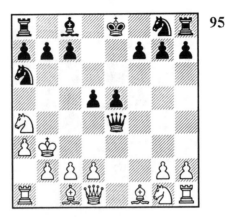

95

Black to move

4

96

White to move

5

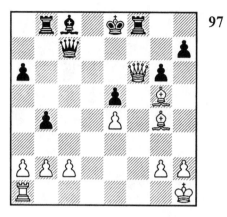

White to move

6

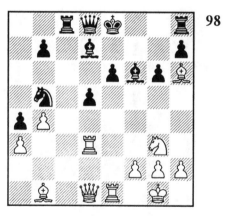

White to move

7

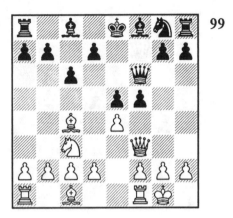

99

White to move

8

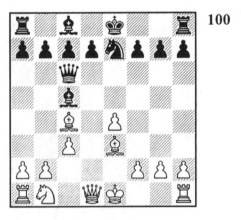

100

White to move

9

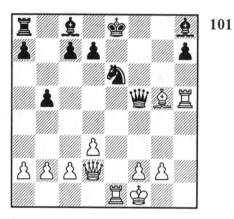

101

White to move

10

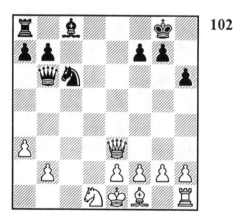

102

Black to move

11

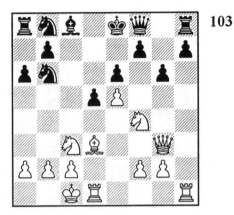

103

White to move

12

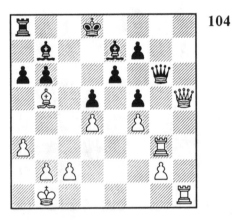

104

Black to move

Solutions

1. *Alekhine — Vasic, Yugoslavia, 1931.* **1. Qxe6+!** — deflecting the f-pawn to clear the diagonal for the decisive move — **1. ... fxe6 2. Bg6 mate.**

2. *Morphy — Stanley, New York, 1857.* This position was reached after 1. e4 e5 2. Nf3 Nc6 3. Bc4 Bc5 4. b4 Bxb4 5. c3 Ba5 6. 0-0 d6 7. d4 exd4 8. cxd4 Bb6 9. Nc3 Nf6 10. e5 dxe5. Now **11. Ba3!** traps the Black king in the center. **11. ... Bxd4 12. Qb3** (with the idea of 13. Bxf7+ and 14. Qe6 mate) **12. ... Be6 13. Bxe6 fxe6 14. Qxe6+ Ne7 15. Nxd4 exd4 16. Rfe1** (now the open e-file and a3-f8 diagonal work together to White's advantage) **16. ... Nfg8 17. Nd5 Qd7 18. Bxe7 Qxe6 19. Rxe6 Kd7 20. Rae1 Re8 21. R6e4** (White now carries his advantage into the endgame) **21. ... c6 22. Rxd4 cxd5 23. Rxd5+ Kc6 24. Rd6+ Kc7 25. Rc1+ Kb8 26. Bh4 Nh6 27. Bg3 Ka8 28. h3 Nf5 29. Rd7 g6 30. Rcc7** and White's domination of the 7th rank was decisive. **He won** after 13 more moves.

3. *Hampe — Meitner, Vienna, 1873.* The opening moves were 1. e4 e5 2. Nc3 Bc5 3. Na4 Bxf2+ 4. Kxf2 Qh4+ 5. Ke3 Qf4+ 6. Kd3 d5 7. Kc3 Qxe4 8. Kb3 Na6 9. a3. Here Black played **9. ... Qxa4+!** (A very interesting pursuit of the White king.) **10. Kxa4 Nc5+ 11. Kb4 a5+ 12. Kxc5 Ne7** (threatening 13. ... b6+ and 14. ... Bd7 mate) **13. Bb5+ Kd8 14. Bc6** (the only defense) **14. ... b6+ 15. Kb5 Nxc6** (threatening 16. ... Nd4+ and 17. ... b5 mate) **16. Kxc6 Bb7+ 17. Kb5** (if 17. Kxb7? White gets mated after 17. ... Kd7 18. Qg4+ Kd6) **17. ... Ba6+ 18. Kc6** (not 18. Ka4? Bc4, followed by 19. ... b5 mate) **18. ... Bb7+ draw** by perpetual check.

4. *Anderssen — Dufresne, Berlin, 1852.* **1. Rad1!** Dufresne played the greedy **1. ... Qxf3.** It looks like Black has everything he could possibly want, but his king is trapped in the center. There followed **2. Rxe7+ Nxe7** (2. ... Kd8 3. Rxd7+ Kxd7 4. Bf5+ Ke8 5. Bd7+ Kd8 6. Bxc6+ Kc8 7. Bd7+ Kd8 8. Be7 mate; or 3. ... Kc8 4. Rd8+! when neither 4. ... Rxd8 5. gxf3 nor 4. ... Nxd8 5. Qd7+! is satisfactory since Black is mated after 5. ... Kxd7 6. Bf5+ Ke8 [or c6] 7. Bd7 mate) **3. Qxd7+!! Kxd7 4. Bf5+ Black resigns** in view of 4. ... Kc6 5. Bd7 mate, or 4. ... Ke8 5. Bd7+ Kd8 (or f8) 6. Bxe7 mate.

5. *Bykhovsky — Lepeshkin, Moscow, 1963.* At first it looks like White's queen is trapped, but White can make use of Black's king in the center with **1. Bd7+! Qxd7** (if instead 1. ... Bxd7 2. Qe7 mate, or 1. ... Kxd7 2. Rd1+ and Rd8+) **2. Qxe5+ Kf7 3. Rf1+ Kg8 4. Rxf8+ Kxf8 5. Qh8+ Kf7 6. Qxh7+ Kf8 7. Bh6+ Ke8 8. Qg8+ Ke7 9. Bg5+ Kd6 10. Qd5+ Kc7 11. Bf4+ Kb6 12. Qxd7 Bxd7 13. Bxb8** and **White won.**

6. *Makarov — Bannik, Ukrainian Championship, 1950.* **1. Rxd5!.** White ignores the fork that this move allows. **1. ... Nc3 2. Qd3 Nxd5?** (relatively better was 2. ... Nxb1) **3. Qxg6+!! hxg6 4. Bxg6+ Ke7 5. Nf5+ mate.**

7. *Bogolyubov — Reti, Stockholm, 1919.* After 1. exf5 Black is ready for counterplay with 1. ... d5, but Bogolyubov uses White's lead in development to attack the king. **1. d4! exd4 2. e5! Qh4** (after 2. ... Qxe5 3. Bg5! Black could resign) **3. Ne2 Bc5 4. b4!** (after this move the bishop must abandon kingside defense and go to b6 since 4. ... Bxb4 5. Qb3 win a piece) **4. ... Bb6 5. g3 Qe4 6. Qb3 Ne7** (Black can resist longer with 6. ... Qxe5 7. Bxg8 d5, but White keeps a big advantage with 8. Bb2! Rxg8 9. Nxd4!) **7. Bg5 h6 8. Bf7+ Kd8 9. Bxe7+ Kxe7 10. Nf4 Black resigns,** since if he saves his rook (10. ... Rh7) he loses his queen (11. Rae1).

8. *Ivanchuk — Gulko, Reykjavik, 1991.* **1. Bxf7+! Kxf7 2. Qh5+ Ng6 3. Qf5+ Ke8** (now Black cannot castle "by hand" with ... Re8) **4. Qxc5 Qxe4 5. Nd2** (after 5. ... Qxg2 6. 0-0-0 all White's pieces are ready to attack) **5. ... Qc6 6. Qh5 d6 7. 0-0 Be6 8. Bd4 Kd7 9. f4 Ne7 10. f5!** (more open lines!) **10. ... Bxf5 11. Rae1 g6 12. Rxe7+** (the decisive combination) **12. ... Kxe7 13. Qg5+ Kd7 14. Bxh8 Qb6+** (after 14. ... Rxh8 White has 15. Rxf5 gxf5 16. Qg7+ and 17. Qxh8) **15. Bd4 Qxb2 16. g4 Be6 17. Rb1 Qxa2 18. Qb5+ Ke7 19. Qxb7 Rd8 20. Rf1** (the final attack) **20. ... Qxd2 21. Qxc7+ Bd7 22. Bf6+ Ke6 23. Qc4+ Black resigns.**

9. *Bogolyubov — Rubinstein, Stockholm, 1920.* This position arose in this famous game after Black's 16th move. **17. Qb4! c5** (Black cannot defend successfully with 17. ... d6 because of 18. g4! Qg6 19. Qxb5+ Bd7 20. Qf5!, or 17. ... Kf7 18. Qe7+ Kg8 19. Rxe6 dxe6 20. Bh6!) **18. Qh4 Kf7 19. Bd8! Qg6 20. Rh6 Qxh6** (or 20. ... Qf5 21. g4 and 22. Qe7+) **21. Qxh6 Nxd8 22. Qh5+ Black resigns.**

10. *Vaganian — Planinc, Hastings, 1974.* **1. ... Nd4! 2. Qe8+ Kh7 3. e3.** (This allows a combination, but White was in trouble anyway — 3. Qxf7 Be6 4. Qf4 Rd8.) **3. ... Nc2+ 4. Kd2 Bf5!!** (drawing

White's queen into the corner) **5. Qxa8 Qd6+ 6. Kc1 Na1!** (threatens ... Nb3 mate) **7. Qxb7 Qc7+!** (deflection—now 8. Qxc7 Nb3 mate) **White resigns.**

11. *Bogolyubov — Spielmann, Stockholm, 1919.* This well known position arose after Black's 14th move. **15. Be4!!.** (Without this sacrifice White can't invade the enemy camp. Black must take the bishop because White threatens 16. Bxd5.) **15. ... dxe4 16. Nxe4 N8d7 17. Qc3! Qe7 18. Nf6+ Nxf6** (18. ... Kf8 19. Nxh7+ Kg7 20. Nh5+ gxh5 21. Qg3+ Kh6 22. Rxh5+!) **19. exf6 Qf8 20. Qc7 Nd7 21. Nd5** (now on 21. ... Qc5? comes 22. Qxc5 Nxc5 23. Nc7+ Kf8 24. Rd8 mate) **21. ... exd5 22. Rhe1+ Ne5 23. Rxe5+ Be6 24. Kb1** (threatening 25. Rdxd5 with mate on d7, as a tempo-winning ... Qh6+ is no longer possible) **24. ... Rd8** (the only way to protect d5) **25. Rdxd5!** (anyway!) **25. ... Rxd5 26. Rxd5 Bxd5 27. Qc8 mate.**

12. *Bogolyubov — Alekhine, New York, 1924.* Position after White's 26th move. This is a good example of successful defense. With **26. ... Qxg3!** Black would be winning — after **27. Qxf7 axb5 28. Rh7** he has the strong reply **28. ... Qe1+ 29. Ka2 Qb4!**, and if **30. Rh8+ Kd7 31. Rxa8** the in-between move **31. ... Qc4+!** leaves White without any chances. In the actual game Black missed his chance with **26. ... Qxh5? 27. Rxh5** and the game ended in a draw on the 85th move.

If the position is closed, then having the king in the center may sometimes even be desirable!

Part II:

Attacks with Same-Side Castling

Lesson Three

Piece Attacks with Same-Side Castling

In Part I, we discussed situations when one side does not castle, focusing especially on cases where a direct attack is possible on the king in the center. But in most games, both players take care to bring their kings to safety by castling.

Now let us discuss one of the critical questions of chess strategy. Is it possible to lead a successful attack on a castled king if the position of the pawns that protect him is strong, and there are no obvious weaknesses?

If we ask the average chess player this question, he is likely to say "no." Many players think that attacking a strongly-defended king accomplishes nothing.

But this conclusion is incorrect!

Even the strongest castled position is not always reliable protection for the king. Of course if there are already weaknesses near your opponent's king, *or if you can create them*, then your attack will develop easier and faster.

We will illustrate these ideas with examples taken from real games. Consider the following position:

Diagram 105
Palatnik — Geller
USSR, 1980

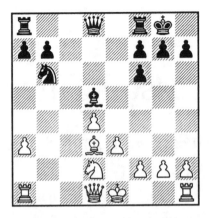

Black to move

15. ...	Bxg2?
16. Rg1	Bc6

On 16. ... Qd5 White plays 17. Qg4 and at the very least wins the bishop on g2.

17. Rxg7+!

Black resigns, since after 17. ... Kxg7 18. Qg4+ Kh8 19. Qf5 mate at h7 is inevitable.

But you can't always count on such cooperation from your opponent every time you want to launch an attack against the castled king! Usually you have to do quite a bit of preparation. Your pieces must be deployed in positions where they can reach the enemy king, and they must be well-coordinated. You should be particularly sensitive to small weaknesses in the enemy's pawn structure, and you should strive to create such weaknesses near his king, even when this requires you to sacrifice material.

When both sides are castled on the same flank, the attack on the enemy king can be conducted either with both pieces and pawns or with just pieces. We can distinguish two main attacking methods: *piece attacks* and *pawn storms.*

Of course an important question to ask is: When should the attack involve pawns, and when should it be led without them? Can we determine the proper role of pawns in an attack with kings castled on the same side? Is there a strategic basis for determining correct attacking methods?

To this question we must reply positively. *The character of an attack is determined by the nature of the position.* We emphasize this idea from the beginning so that it will be in your mind as you study the following lessons.

Let's move on to some specific examples, and as we go along we will make useful comments and draw conclusions. Our introductory game is a kingside pawn attack by Steinitz that demonstrates the correct application of attacking ideas. Subsequent examples will distinguish between cases when a pawn attack is appropriate, and when it is best to attack only with pieces.

The stronger side must attack!

Steinitz — MacDonnell
Dublin, 1865

1. e4 e5 2. Nf3 d6 3. Bc4 Be7 4. c3 Nf6 5. d3 0-0 6. 0-0 Bg4 7. h3 Bxf3

Black's plan of exchanging his light-squared bishop isn't good. White now has two strong bishops, one of them unopposed.

8. Qxf3	c6
9. Bb3	Nbd7
10. Qe2	Nc5
11. Bc2	Ne6
12. g3	Qc7

Diagram 106

The purpose of Black's last move was to regroup and prepare for central expansion with moves like ... Rad8 and ... d6-d5. If he had enough time, he would eventually achieve harmony among his forces. But now it is White's move! At this moment White correctly decides he has the advantage and he must react energetically to stop Black's consolidation.

Steinitz observed that in situations where one side has an advantage and can point to clear reasons for starting an attack, he should attack. Otherwise the advantage will just evaporate.

There is nothing odd about this principle. It is logical that if your pieces are harmoniously placed and ready for an attack, you must find a way to take advantage of this; otherwise, your opponent will make his position better and you will lose your advantage and your chance to attack.

So the moment has arrived in this game where the stronger side not only *can* be active, but *must* be active. With his last move, White started an attack on Black's king.

Steinitz also said that *the attack should always be focused on the weakest square in the opponent's position.* Here Black's kingside is vulnerable because White can take immediate steps to increase his space advantage there. White also has a strong position in the center, which is essential before starting a pawn advance on the side. This game is a good example of how a stable position in the center can allow one side to attack with pawns and to open lines against the enemy king.

13. f4

Diagram 107

This is the first flash of lightning in the pawn storm. The idea is to drive the defending forces (knights) away from their posts and seize space on the kingside.

13. ...	Rfe8
14. Nd2	Rad8
15. Nf3	Kh8
16. f5	Nf8
17. g4	

Diagram 108

17. ...   h6?

This makes life easier for White, because now he can open lines against Black's king. *In general, try not to move pawns in an area where you are weak (especially close to your king)!*

18. g5	hxg5
19. Nxg5	Kg8
20. Kh1	N6h7
21. Nf3	

Diagram 109

The attacking side usually tries to avoid exchanges, which tend to dilute the strength of the attack. More specifically, the attacker is willing to trade a non-attacking piece for a defending piece, while the defender wants to exchange off as many attackers as possible to limit the force of the attack.

By keeping his pieces on the board, Steinitz soon crashes through his opponent's position.

21. ... Rd7 22. Rg1 Bd8 23. Bh6 f6 24. Rg2 d5 25. Rag1 Ree7 26. exd5 cxd5

Diagram 110

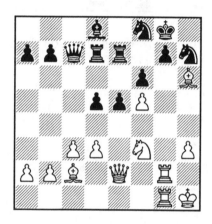

27. Ba4

Winning material.

27. ... Rd6 28. Rxg7+ Rxg7 29. Rxg7+ Qxg7 30. Bxg7

And White went on to realize his material advantage.

Piece attacks against weak pawn structure

Target on g6

Spielmann — Honlinger
Vienna, 1927

1. e4 c6 2. d4 d5 3. Nc3 dxe4 4. Nxe4 Nf6 5. Ng3 e6 6. Nf3 c5 7. Bd3 Nc6 8. dxc5 Bxc5 9. a3

Diagram 111

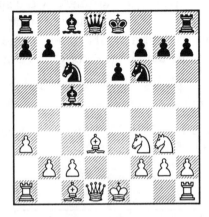

White's last move preserves the Bd3 from exchange by ... Nb4, and also prepares b2-b4 and Bb2.

9. ...	0-0
10. 0-0	b6
11. b4	Be7
12. Bb2	

White aims his pieces at Black's kingside while keeping a firm grip on the e5-square.

Diagram 112

| 12. ... | Qc7 |
| 13. b5 | Na5 |

Safer is 13. ... Nb8 in order to bring the knight back into action via d7. On a5 the knight will be out of play for a long time.

14. Ne5	Bb7
15. Ng4	Qd8
16. Ne3	Nd5?

This allows White's queen to reach the kingside — with decisive effect.

| 17. Qh5! | g6 |

On 17. ... f5 White wins with 18. Ngxf5, and 17. ... h6 allows 18. Bxg7! Kxg7 19. Ngf5+ exf5 20. Nxf5+ and 21. Qxh6 with a quick mate.

Diagram 113

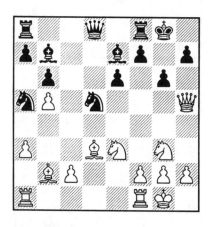

| 18. Ng4!! | Bf6 |

Too many pieces are aimed against Black's king for a successful defense to be possible. If 18. ... f6 19. Bxg6 hxg6 20. Qxg6+ Kh8 21. Nh5 and mates; or 18. ... Nf6 19. Qe5! Kg7 20. Nxf6 Bxf6 21. Nh5+ gxh5 22. Qg5+ winning. And of course not 18. ... gxh5 19. Nh6 mate.

| 19. Nxf6+ | |

After exchanging away Black's dark-square bishop, White's pressure on the long diagonal soon becomes overwhelming.

19. ...	Nxf6
20. Qh6	Rc8
21. Rad1	Qe7
22. Rfe1	Ne8

Diagram 114

| **23. Nf5!** | **Qc5** |

If 23. ... gxf5 24. Bxf5 f6 25. Bxe6+ Kh8 26. Rd7.

| **24. Re5** | **Bd5** |

Diagram 115

Now White mates in four moves: **25. Ne7+! Qxe7 26. Qxh7+ Kxh7 27. Rh5+ Kg8 28. Rh8 mate.**

Target on h6

Diagram 116
Capablanca — Levenfish
Moscow, 1935

Position after Black's 16th move

The immediate 17. Nc6 does not work because of 17. ... Bb7. This suggests a queen move for White, preferably an aggressive one.

17. Qh3!

Now the threat of 18. Nc6 is real.

17. ...	Rc5
18. Rxc5	Bxc5
19. Bg5	

Do you notice the pattern? Once the White queen and bishop are lined up against h7, Black's Nf6 is the only piece holding Black's game together. To avoid mate Black must weaken his kingside with either ... g6 or ... h6. (In this position, either is fatal.)

19. ...	h6

Or 19. ... g6 20. Nc6! Qd5 21. Bxf6 Qxc6 22. Qh6 followed by 23. Qg7 mate.

Diagram 117

20. Ng4!

Also possible is 20. Bxh6, but Capablanca's move is stronger.

20. ...	Be7
21. Bxf6	

But here more precise would be 21. Nxh6+ gxh6 22. Bxf6 transposing into the next note.

21. ...	gxf6

After 21. ... Bxf6 22. Nxh6+ gxh6 23. Qxh6, another typical mating pattern occurs: 23. ... Re8 24. Bh7+! Kh8 25. Bg6+ Kg8 26. Qh7+ Kf8 27. Qxf7 mate.

22. Nxh6+	Kg7
23. Qg4+	Kh8

If 23. ... Kxh6 24. Qh4+ Kg7 25. Qh7 mate.

24. Qh5	Kg7
25. Nxf7	

Diagram 118

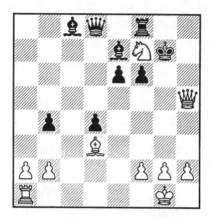

25. ...	**Rh8**

No better is 25. ... Rxf7 26. Qh7+ Kf8 27. Qh8 mate.

26. Qg6+	**Black resigns.**

Invading weak squares

Diagram 119
Alatortsev—Boleslavsky
XVIIIth USSR Championship, 1950

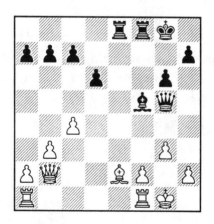

Position after White's 19th move

The position of White's king is weakened because of the pawn on g3, and this weakening is even more serious because Black still has a light-squared bishop on the board. In keeping with Steinitz's principle, Black's main idea is to organize an immediate attack against the weakest squares in White's position — h3 and g2.

19. ...   Bh3
20. f4

What would have happened if White moved his rook? Let's try some sample lines:

1) *20. Rfe1* then 20. ... Rxf2!, and White cannot play 21. Kxf2? because of 21. ... Qe3 mate.

2) *20. Rfc1* Rxf2 (anyway!) 21. Kxf2 Qe3+ 22. Ke1 Qg1+ 23. Kd2 Rxe2+ 24. Kxe2 Qxh2+ winning the queen.

3) *20. Rfb1* (to protect the queen), but then 20. ... Rxf2 21. Kxf2 Qe3+ 22. Ke1 Bg4 (threatening 23. ... Qg1+ and 24. ... Rxe2+) 23. Kf1 Rf8+ 24. Ke1 Rf2.

By playing 20. f4, White hoped to organize a successful defense after the "obvious" 20. ... Qc5+ 21. Rf2 followed by Bf1-g2.

20. ...   Bxf1!

A brilliant move! By sacrificing the queen Black weakens White's position to the maximum extent, and begins an unstoppable attack.

21. fxg5   Rxe2

Diagram 120

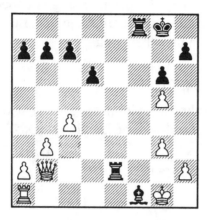

22. Qc3

Among White's alternatives 22. Qd4 is the most active, and the only one requiring analysis. After 22. Qd4 Bh3 23. Qh4 (Black threatened 23. ... Rg2+ 24. Kh1 Rgf2 followed by mate on f1—if 23. Qd5+ then 23. ... Rf7 with the idea of playing 24. ... Rf2 and White's queen could not simultaneously control both f2 and g2), GM Boleslavsky recommends continuing with 23. ... Bg2, but it is also possible immediately to enter the technical phase of the game with 23. ... Rg2+ 24. Kh1 Rxa2, when best for White is 25. Qxh3 (25. Rxa2 Rf1 mate) 25. ... Rxa1+ 26. Kg2, but after 26. ... Ra2+ 27. Kg1 Rf5 Black will have a winning advantage. If White does not take the rook on a2 or the bishop, then the bishop will be transferred via g2 or d7 to c6 with decisive effect—for example, 25. Re1 Bg2+ 26. Kg1 Bc6 27. Qh3 Rf5, and White is completely helpless because the queen has to protect the g2-square and the rook has to protect the first rank. At the right moment, Black can go into a rook ending with two extra pawns by playing ... Rg2+.

22. ...   Bg2

The threat is 23. ... Bc6 followed by ... Rg2+ and a deadly discovered check. On 23. Re1 Black could respond 23. ... Bh3 to achieve a winning pawn ending after the exchange of rooks

on e1 and check on f1. If White responds 24. Rd1, then 24. ...
Ref2 25. Qd3 Rf1+. The pawn ending is hopeless for White
because his kingside pawns are disabled and Black has a healthy
pawn majority on the other wing.

| 23. Qd3 | Bf3 |
| 24. Rf1 | |

A mistake leading to an immediate loss, but White's position
is already indefensible—for example, 24. Qd4 Bc6.

| 24. ... | Rg2+ |
| 25. Kh1 | Bc6! |

Diagram 121

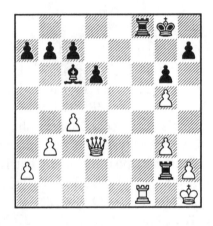

26. Rxf8+	Kxf8
27. Qf1+	Rf2+
White resigns.	

Take a moment to return to the starting diagram of this game
(Alatortsev — Boleslavsky). We started out by saying that
White's kingside was weakened by the move g2-g3. But isn't
Black's kingside also weakened? Why is Black winning in this
position in spite of having the same type of weakness?

The most important factor here is not the weakness itself, but
the possibilities for exploiting the weakness. Black is well

placed to take advantage of his opponent's weak squares on the kingside in a way that White is not.

White lost not only because his castled position was weakened, but also because the Black pieces worked well together in attacking White's king. That means that the weaknesses of the squares h3 and g2 were not only real in a theoretical sense, but also played a decisive role in the dynamic struggle that followed.

The weakness of White's position originates in White's inability to create either attack or defense because his uncoordinated pieces are scattered all over the board. Make a simple change in the initial position — move the bishop from e2 to g2, for example — and the situation would immediately change. Now we can better understand the wisdom in Steinitz's principle that we must act quickly or see our temporary advantages disappear.

In this last example we saw a clear piece attack that became stronger with the help of a sacrifice. By making this sacrifice, Black opened the position of the enemy king even more, and the remaining pieces were sufficient for a winning attack.

Diagram 122
Smyslov— Stahlberg
Zurich, 1953

Position after Black's 18th move

The pawn structure near Black's king is weakened, and Black lacks counterplay. These facts allow Smyslov quickly to create an attack, which after only a couple of moves brings him a decisive material advantage.

19. Qe3

The strongest piece aims at the weakest square (h6) in Black's position. Favoring White is 19. ... Nxc4 20. Qh6— for example, 20. ... Qe7 21. Rd3 Kh8 (the threat was 22. Ne5, and 21. ... Nd6 will be followed by 22. Nh4 Kh8 23. Rh3) 22. Nh4 Rd5 23. Nf5. Or if 20. ... Rd5 21. Re4 (stronger than 21. Qxf6, when Black has resources such as 21. ... Rf5 and 22. ... Qf4) 21. ... f5 22. Ng5 f6 23. Qxf8+ winning the Exchange.

19. ...   Kg7

How can White attack the kingside now? He must act quickly because Black will soon bring more pieces to the defense, for example with ... Nd7.

Diagram 123

20. Ne5!

This is the answer. The threat is 21. Ng4 followed by 22. Qh6+. Black cannot take the knight because 20. ... fxe5 21. Qg5+ Kh8 22. Qf6+ Kg8 23. Rxe5 Rfe8 24. Rh5 with the threat 25. Rxh7, for example—24. ... Nd7 25. Qg5+ Kf8 26. Rxh7 or 24. ... e5 25. Rxh7 Kxh7 26. Rd3 Qc8 27. Rg3 Rg8 28. Qh4 mate.

20. ...   Qe7

Or 20. ... h5, 21. Qg3+ Kh7 (else he loses the queen) 22. Qh4 fxe5 23. Qxh5+ Kg7 24. Qg5+ and 25. Re3. Black is unable to prevent White from invading on h6, and this decides the game.

21. Ng4   Rfg8
22. Nh6

Diagram 124

This move wins the Exchange, which here is sufficient for a win. From a practical point of view, such a decision often turns out to be the most effective way to win.

Trying for more with 21. Qh6+ Kh8 22. Nxf6 Rg7 23. Re3 with the threat of 24. Rh3 and 25. Qxh7+, as well as 24. Rg3, would be defended by 23. ... Nd7.

22. ...   Qc7

If 22. ... Nxc4, then 23. Nf5+ Kh8 24. Qh6 Rg6 25. Qxg6 hxg6 26. Nxe7.

23. Nxg8   Rxg8

Diagram 125

Smyslov went on to win this game with his usual precision:
24. b3 Kh8 25. Qh6 Rg6 26. Qh4 Nd7 27. Re3 Qa5 28. Rh3 Nf8 29. Rg3 Qxa2 30. Rxg6 Nxg6 31. Qxf6+ Kg8 32. Qf3 Qc2 33. Qd3 Black resigns.

Lack of harmony

Diagram 126
Kasparov — Marjanovic
Malta, 1980

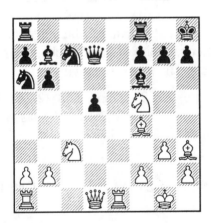

Position after Black's 16th move

17. Ne4!

White's attack cannot be repulsed because he has a decisive concentration of force against Black's kingside.

17. ...	Bxb2
18. Ng5	Qc6

Against 18. ... Ne6 the easiest win is 19. Nd6 with the threat of 20. Qc2.

19. Ne7	Qf6

Diagram 127

20. Nxh7!	Qd4
21. Qh5	g6
22. Qh4	Bxa1
23. Nf6+	Black resigns.

The finish would be 23. ... Kg7 24. Qh6+ Kxf6 25. Bg5 mate.

Diagram 128
Kasparov — Pribyl
Skara, 1980

Position after Black's 25th move

26. d8=Q!

A paradoxical move. Earlier in this game White was mainly concerned with creating and advancing this pawn. But now he sacrifices it in order to create a decisive lack of coordination among the Black forces.

| 26. ... | Bxd8 |

Also bad is 26. ... Rxd8 27. Rxd8+ Bxd8 28. Qf7 (threatening 29. Qf8 mate), and if 28. ... Qd5 White has 29. Qxd5 Nxd5 30. Rd1, with extra material.

27. Qc3+	Kg8
28. Rd7	Bf6
29. Qc4+	Kh8
30. Qf4	

White wins a piece. The best defense was 30. ... Bg7 31. Qxc7 Qxc7 32. Rxc7 Bd4 33. Rf1, and White should still win this endgame, but not without difficulty. Instead, Black chooses a move that loses instantly.

Diagram 129

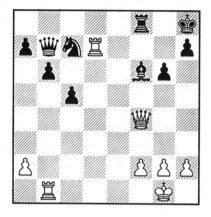

| 30. ... | Qa6? |

Now there is no defense to mate.

| **31. Qh6** | **Black resigns.** |

Weak diagonal

Diagram 130
Alekhine — Alexander
Nottingham, 1936

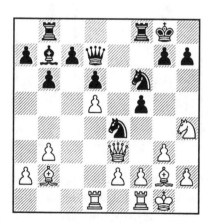

Position after Black's 15th move

In evaluating this position, we can immediately notice the strong bishop at b2, striking unopposed at Black's kingside. Black also has two potential weaknesses at c7 and e6.

On the other hand, it is not easy for White to exploit his opponent's weak points, and the first player must also take care to guard his own weakness at d5.

Is there a way for White to defend his d5-pawn without the exchange Bxf6, reducing his attacking chances? Alekhine found such a plan, allowing him to create additional weaknesses around Black's king while retaining the powerful Bb2 for the attack.

16. Bh3!

This move indirectly protects the d-pawn, because 16. ... Nxd5? 17. Qxe4 or 16. ... Bxd5 17. Rxd5 Nxd5 18. Qxe4 favors White.

16. ...   g6

Diagram 131

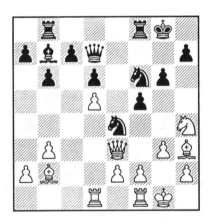

Black's last move greatly increased the scope of the bishop on b2, and White can now think about attacking the Black king. But what plan should he follow, and how can he use weaknesses in the opponent's position?

White's pieces are not yet sufficiently coordinated for an attack. So he must open up the game to increase the activity of his pieces, concentrating them in an attack on the opponent's king.

What should White do first? His bishop on b2 is definitely looking toward the kingside, but the position of his other bishop and the knight on h4 could be improved by removing the f5-pawn that restricts them. Also, Black's knight on e4 reduces the harmony of White's forces — no active operations will be possible until this piece is driven back.

In order to achieve these aims, White drives out the annoying knight with f3, and soon follows up with the thrust e2-e4. His plan leads to the immediate activation of his own pieces as well as the scattering of Black's forces.

| 17. f3 | Nc5 |
| 18. Qg5 | |

White not only clears the way for the advance of the e-pawn but also moves his strongest piece to the kingside, creating powerful threats. The knight on f6 and the pawn on f5 will be under attack, and on 18. ... Nxd5 the answer would be 19. Nxg6!.

| 18. ... | Qg7 |
| 19. b4 | |

This drives the Black knight away from covering e4 so that White's e2-e4 plan can become a reality.

| 19. ... | Ncd7 |

After 19. ... Na4 20. Ba1 this knight would be out of the game.

Diagram 132

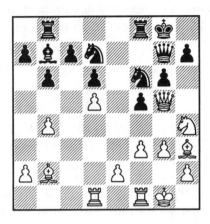

20. e4!

The point is that 20. ... fxe4 loses a piece to 21. Bxd7. Black must have relied on his next move, but Alekhine has seen more deeply into the position.

20. ...   Nxe4

If now 21. Bxg7, then 21. ... Nxg5 22. Bxf8 Nxh3+ 23. Kg2 Rxf8 24. Kxh3 Nf6, and Black wins a second pawn for the Exchange, with an excellent endgame. This was Alexander's main idea. But Alekhine replied ...

21. Qc1!   Nef6
22. Bxf5!

Diagram 133

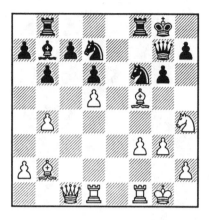

This move is the point. Black cannot take the bishop because of 23. Nxf5 Qh8 (or he loses the queen) 24. Nh6+ Kg7 25. Qg5 mate. So the important f5-pawn is gone, and White not only keeps his main fighting piece (the bishop on b2) but now the other bishop will go to e6 and take an active part in the attack.

| 22. ... | Kh8 |
| 23. Be6 | Ba6 |

Black's problems are not limited to the long diagonal — he must also protect the c7-pawn. However, if 23. ... Rbc8, White wins with 24. g4, and if 23. ... Ne5 24. f4.

| 24. Rfe1 | Ne5 |
| 25. f4! | |

Clearing the a1-h8 diagonal.

25. ...	Nd3
26. Rxd3!	Bxd3
27. g4	

In general, try not to move pawns in an area where you are weak (especially close to your king)!

Diagram 134

Now there is no defense to 28. g5, so **Black resigns**.

What can we say about the character of the attack in this example? What role did the White pawns play in it?

White's central pawn advance not only opened up the game for his two bishops, but also exposed Black's king and made White's pieces more active. The forced weakness, g7-g6, was enough to create a winning piece attack. The final pawn advance g3-g4 was only the final tactical move. Pawns played a big part in White's strategic plan, but they did not participate in weakening Black's castled position, nor in the attack on the king.

* * * * *

So far we have seen examples in which piece attacks against weakened castled positions were made when both sides castled short. But how do we attack when both sides castle long?

Basically there is no difference between these two kinds of attacks. The only important difference is that after castling long the king usually stays on c1 or c8. Attacks on the queenside castled position are usually easier to develop than a similar attack on the kingside. The explanation for this is that the pieces do not naturally protect the queenside pawns as well as they do the kingside pawns.

In all of the games we have analysed so far, the active side succeeded by being better coordinated than the opponent. So far our examples have shown how to exploit big weaknesses in the opponent's kingside. When the winning attack is carried out by pieces alone, a breakthrough is achieved by sacrifices to expose the enemy king.

Before we examine piece attacks against a king whose pawn cover is strong, we would like to show you the tragic consequences of attacking from a position where the pieces are not acting in harmony, even though the opponent's position contains pawn weaknesses.

Unprepared attack

Diagram 135
Capablanca — Becker
Carlsbad, 1929

Position after White's 14th move

White's pawn position contains weaknesses — but can Black exploit them? We have already mentioned that pawn weaknesses should be treated only as one part of the overall picture.

Think of it this way: What are the positive aspects of White's position?

First of all, it is not hard to see that White is completely mobilized, with all of his pieces on good squares. Black's rooks are not ready for action. In addition White has the advantage in the center because he controls every square except d5.

Black simply does not have a sufficiently aggressive placement of his pieces to launch a successful assault based on his structural advantage. Instead, Black should aim to hold the balance for now, and look for success in the endgame.

Black could have continued 14. ... Qe7, with the idea of ... Rfd8, leading to a balanced game, but he decided instead to try to seize the initiative with the hope of creating an attack. This mistaken idea quickly gives Black a losing game.

| **14. ...** | **Bb4** |

Black wants to play ... Bxc3 followed by ... Qd5.

| **15. Ne4** | **Qd5** |

Now after 16. Nxf6+ gxf6, Black will have a dangerous battery on the main diagonal. However, an attack in which only two pieces take part (queen and the bishop) can be easily defended by White's superior forces.

16. Nfg5!

Diagram 136

Suddenly Black is in grave danger. White threatens 17. Nxf6+ gxf6 18. Be4, and the pawn on c7 is also under attack. Black does not have a satisfactory defense; for example, 16. ... Kh8 17. Rxc7 and the threat is not only 18. Bc4 winning the bishop, but also 18. Rxb7 Qxb7 19. Nxf6 gxf6 20. Qh5 and checkmate.

16. ...	Ne8
17. Nxh7!	f5
18. Nhg5!	

This is stronger than taking the rook. On 18. ... fxe4 White wins by 19. Bxe4; otherwise, White will play 19. Qh5 or 19. Bc4, so **Black resigns**. A very instructive example.

Piece attacks against strong pawn structure

Now let's turn our attention to the topic of piece attacks against castled positions with no obvious weaknesses.

Combination to increase activity

Diagram 137
Euwe — Keres
The Hague, 1948

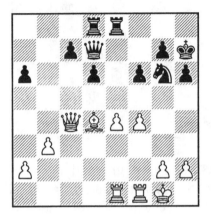

Position after White's 28th move

White's situation on the kingside looks very strong — he has more space and his king appears safe.

Again, what is important is not the weaknesses themselves, but how well you can exploit them. In this particular situation, the weakness of Black's pawns on the kingside is not a real problem for him. It would be a different story if the White bishop were on c2 instead of d4.

Black starts with a small combination that allows his pieces to assume good attacking positions.

28. ...	Rxe4!
29. Rxe4	d5
30. Qxa6	dxe4
31. Be3	Qg4!

Diagram 138

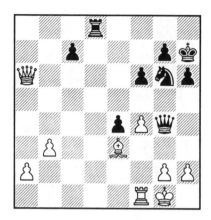

The initial combination is over, and now we can see how well the Black pieces work together. Black's queen and knight are ready to attack g2, and the rook controls the open center file. Plus, Black's advanced center pawn can support an invasion by his pieces.

32. Qc4

After 32. h3 Qg3 33. Qe2 Nh4, the threat of 34. ... Nf3+ is highly unpleasant.

32. ...	**Rd3!**

Now White cannot take the pawn on e4 because of 33. ... Qe2 winning a piece. On 33. Re1 Black would simply answer 33. ... f5, and after that there would not be any defense against 34. ... Nxf4 or 34. ... Nh4.

33. Bc1	**Nh4!**

Diagram 139

34. Qxe4+

White accepts the pawn sacrifice. The passive defense 34. Qc2 would lead to a bad position after 34. ... f5, when Black has a strong position with no risk.

34. ...   **f5**
35. Qb7

White is forced to move his queen away. If 35. Qc6 Rc3.

35. ...   **c6**

Diagram 140

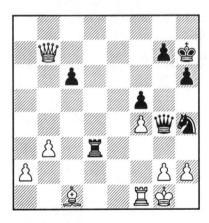

By this point both opponents were in time trouble. Keres thinks that it would have been better to play 35. ... Rc3 with the threat 36. ... c6, cutting off the queen from the defense of the g2-square.

| 36. Qxc6 | Rc3! |
| 37. Qd5 | Rc5! |

Black forces the queen back, with the idea of answering 38. Qb7 with 38. ... Rc2, when White would not have the defense 39. Bd2.

38. Qd2

Diagram 141

| 38. ... | Rxc1! |

White cannot take the rook and therefore loses a piece.

39. h3?

A big mistake. After 39. Qf2 Black would still have some hard work to do.

| 39. ... | Qg3? |

Returning the favor. Of course 39. ... Nf3+ instead would immediately decide the game.

| 40. Qe2 | Qxf4 |

Diagram 142

With time trouble over, the rest was not difficult: **41. Rxc1 Qxc1+ 42. Kh2 Qf4+ 43. Kg1 Ng6 44. Qc2 Ne7 45. a4 Qd4+ 46. Kh2 Qe5+ 47. Kg1 Nd5 48. Qd1 Nc3 49. Qc2 Kg6 50. Kh1 Qe1+ 51. Kh2 Ne2 52. Qc6+ Kh7 53. Qc5 Ng3 54. Qd6 Nf1+ 55. Kg1 h5, and White lost on time.**

Exchanging to increase activity

Diagram 143
Tal — Najdorf
Budapest, 1960

Position after Black's 14th move

It is interesting to see how, just by making simple exchanges, the world champion creates a strong attacking position. Even though the Black king has a strong pawn wall, he will be in a very difficult situation.

| 15. exd5! | Nxd3 |

Of course Black needs to exchange this dangerous bishop.

| 16. cxd3 | Bxd5 |

It turns out that the "normal" move 16. ... Nxd5 leads to material loss after 17. Nxe6. If Black takes on d5 with a pawn, he would have a "bad" bishop on b7, blocked by his own pawn.

| 17. Nxd5 | exd5 |
| 18. Nf5 | |

Diagram 144

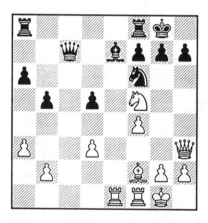

A signal to attack. White already has a queen, rook, and knight aimed at Black's kingside, and Black does not have adequate resources for defense.

| 18. ... | Bc5 |

After 18. ... Rfe8 19. Qg3 Bf8. (If 19. ... Nh5 then 20. Qf3. It is not good to play 19. ... g6 because of 20. Qg5 Bd8 21. Bd4.) 20. Bd4 and White has a strong attacking position.

| 19. d4 | Ba7 |
| 20. Bh4 | Ne4 |

Diagram 145

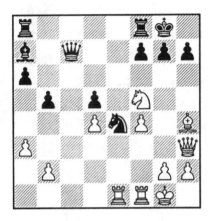

21. Rxe4!

By sacrificing the Exchange, White liquidates an important defender and achieves a decisive advantage in the number of pieces attacking the Black king

21. ...	dxe4
22. Bf6!	Qb6
23. Bxg7	Rfe8
24. Be5	

Diagram 146

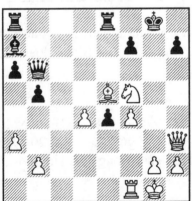

Black's king is now open for a direct assault. The threat is 25. Nh6+ Kf8 26. Nxf7, winning another pawn while continuing the attack. The knight can't be taken: 26. ... Kxf7 27. Qxh7+ Ke6 28. f5+ Kd5 29. Qf7+ Kc6 30. Rc1+.

| 24. ... | Qg6 |

If 24. ... Re6, then 25. Qg4+ Rg6 26. Ne7+ Kf8 27. Nxg6+. On 24. ... Qe6 it would be good to play 25. Nh6+ Kf8 26. Ng4 with many strong threats.

| 25. Nh6+ | Kf8 |
| 26. f5 | Black resigns. |

Diagram 147

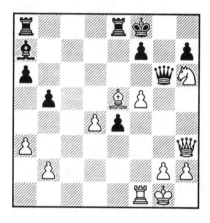

Black has no good moves. If 26. ... Qg5 27. Nxf7! wins, and after 26. ... Qc6 27. Qh5 Re7 28. f6 Rb7 29. Nf5, the Black king cannot escape.

Sacrifice to divert defenders

Diagram 148
Alekhine — Sterk
Budapest, 1921

Position after Black's 15th move

Our study of piece attacks against a strong kingside pawn formation continues with another inspired example from Alekhine. This game is noteworthy, not only because of the former world champion's excellent technique, but also because of the wonderful way in which the attack is prepared. By sacrificing a pawn, Alekhine was able to divert nearly all of his opponent's pieces from the defense of their king.

The game continued **16. Bd3 Bxc3 17. Rfc1! Nxe4 18. Bxe4 Bxe4 19. Qxe4 Nc5 20. Qe2! Ba5 21. Rab1 Qa6 22. Rc4 Na4**

Diagram 149

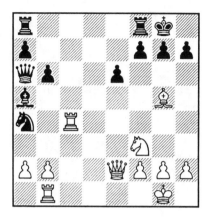

Since Black's pieces are all on the queenside, Alekhine starts an attack on the opposite side of the board.

White cannot continue with 23. b4 because of the reply 23. ... Nc3, and White must also watch out for Black's threat 23. ... Rac8, exploiting the pin on his rook.

23. Bf6!

White's bishop is immune — if 23. ... gxf6 24. Rg4+ wins the queen.

23. ...   Rfc8
24. Qe5!

What's important is not the weaknesses themselves—but how well you exploit them!

Diagram 150

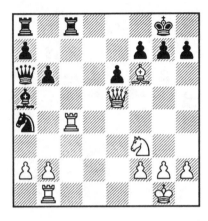

Black must defend against 25. Qg5 as well as 25. Rg4, and so he cannot capture either the rook or the bishop.

24. ...	**Rc5**
25. Qg3!	

Winning a knight. After **25. ... g6 26. Rxa4 Qd3 27. Rf1 Qf5 28. Qf4 Qc2 29. Qh6 Black resigns**.

The importance of greater activity in piece attacks

So far we have seen that it *is possible* to lead a successful attack on a castled position that has no obvious weaknesses. When the attack involves only pieces, the activity of the attacker's forces is the most important factor. Usually the active side either forces the opponent to weaken his king's position and then develops an attack, or by sacrificing material the active side opens up the defending king's position and then, with his remaining forces, lands the winning blow.

So far we have seen only attacks with pieces. A natural question arises: Why didn't pawns take part in the attack? The answer is that they did not do so *because the character of the position did not require it.*

Open and closed positions

If we carefully go back through the preceding positions, we would find that they were essentially *open positions*. In each case there were many open ranks, files, and diagonals providing pieces with great maneuverability. Also the center of the board was not blocked by pawns. This is in contrast to closed positions, where the center is often blocked by pawns and there are few, if any, open files.

There are no absolute rules on how to distinguish between open and closed positions. However, with some experience, a chess player can determine whether the dominant character of the position is open or closed.

In open positions, flank pawns are not usually advanced for attacking purposes, as demonstrated in the preceding examples.

In conducting a piece attack using well coordinated forces, the active side in open positions does not need any extra opening of the game, and so the participation of pawns in the attack is unnecessary. This is one side of the question.

Besides, in piece attacks involving castling on the same side, the attacker does not usually have to worry about his own king because he is protected by his pawns, and the activity of his own pieces on that flank will probably eliminate any chances for counterattack. But if the pawns also participate in the attack, then the king's position opens up, and the chance of a successful counterattack increases.

Counterattack

A counterattack can be very unpleasant for the attacker, especially when it involves the center, because pieces in the center are more active. So we must pay special attention to our control of the central squares when moving pawns in front of our own king. If the opponent has the possibility of taking direct action in the center, then pawn moves that open our own king will be much riskier.

Therefore, *if the kings are castled on the same side and one of the sides is attacking, the pawns join the attack only when the position is closed* and it is hard for the opponent to organize a counterattack.

Another important question is how to evaluate a counterattack on the other side of the board.

Consider the following game situation: The center is closed, you are making a kingside attack by advancing pawns there, and your opponent is attacking the queenside (also by advancing pawns). Under some conditions he may be able to break through on the other side of the board before you do. This can create a difficult situation, because your opponent may invade your first two ranks with heavy pieces, and his invasion may create threats that are difficult to stop if your pieces are far away in attacking positions and unable to come to the defense.

If we attack the enemy king using only one pawn rather than a full-scale pawn advance, the resulting weakness in our king's position is diminished, and we decrease the chances of a successful counterattack. It is thus possible to attack using only one pawn when the position is open in character.

Attacks in which only one pawn participates usually feature either a rook's pawn or a bishop's pawn. Advancing one of these pawns weakens our kingside slightly, but not nearly as much as if we advance the knight's pawn. Moving the knight's pawn creates more weak squares than the other pawns.

Again we emphasize that *the decisive role in such situations is not played by the weaknesses themselves, but in how you take advantage of them.* This is why the role of weaknesses can be different, depending on the concrete situation.

In the next game, White started a strong attack on the king and sacrificed a pawn. Geller would have had good chances for success if Black had not made a timely counterattack on the queenside.

Euwe employed two wonderful ideas: 1) Use the open lines from a *queenside counterattack* as the basis for an attack on the opponent's kingside; and 2) Tempt the opponent's pieces to advance with the idea of separating them from the defense of their own king. It is interesting to watch how White's pieces move further and further into Black's position, until they finally reach a point from which there is no coming back!

Successful counterattack against overextended attacker

Diagram 151
Geller — Euwe
Zurich, 1953

1. d4 Nf6 2. c4 e6 3. Nc3 Bb4 4. e3 c5 5. a3 Bxc3+ 6. bxc3 b6 7. Bd3 Bb7 8. f3 Nc6 9. Ne2 0-0 10. 0-0 Na5 11. e4 Ne8

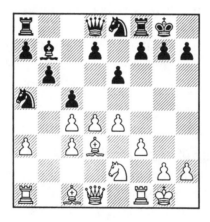

Black moved his knight to avoid being pinned by Bg5, and also to be able to reply to the move f3-f4 with ... f7-f5, blocking the kingside. That is why, before White moves his f-pawn, he takes the f5-square under control. There is no reason for White to worry about protecting the c4-pawn: in this sharp position, advancing on the kingside is more important. Besides, the c4-pawn was already doomed by White's fifth move.

12. Ng3 cxd4 13. cxd4 Rc8 14. f4 Nxc4 15. f5 f6

Diagram 152

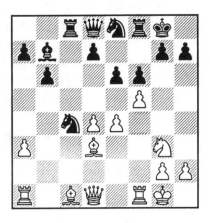

16. Rf4

White's attack has become most threatening. Black's last move (... f7-f6) was necessary because otherwise White would advance his pawn to f6. In answer to ... Nxf6, White would pin the knight (Bc1-g5) and then open Black's kingside. Now after 16. Rf4, White needs only two moves to transfer his queen and rook to the h-file, after which it looks like nothing will save the Black king.

16. ...	b5!

The beginning of an excellent plan. Any kind of defense on the kingside with moves like ... Rf7 or ... Qe7 is useless since these pieces have a very limited range of action. But Black has another plan — counterattack! The Black bishop on b7, the rook on c8, and the knight on c4 all occupy good squares. The only piece left out right now is the queen. The basis of the counterattack is Black's control of the central dark squares. By playing ... b6-b5, Black makes his knight's position more secure and opens a path for his queen to b6. But it looks like Black's idea comes too late.

17. Rh4	Qb6

By tying White's queen to the defense of the d4 pawn, Black stops Qh5 for the moment. But if instead White had played 17. Qh5 Qb6 18. Ne2 Ne5, it would be too late to play 19. Rh4 because the bishop on d3 is under attack.

18. e5	Nxe5
19. fxe6	Nxd3
20. Qxd3	

All of White's moves required exact calculation. For example, now it would not be good to play 20. exd7 because of 20. ... Qc6.

20. ...	Qxe6
21. Qxh7+	

So by paying a small price, White has broken through. Black's position seems critical.

21. ...	Kf7
22. Bh6	

Diagram 153

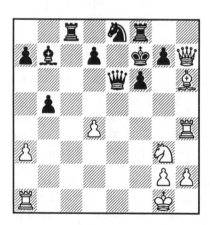

22. ...	Rh8

If Black's 16th move was the begining of a strategic plan of counterattack, then this rook sacrifice is the central tactical stroke. The idea is to deflect White's queen from the c2-square.

23. Qxh8	**Rc2**

Diagram 154

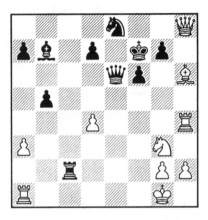

Black's threat is checkmate in a couple of moves with 24. ... Rxg2+, 25. ... Qc4+, etc.

24. Rac1

A very difficult analysis shows that White could have avoided checkmate by making a couple of forced moves. He should have played 24. d5!; e.g. 24. ... Qb6+ 25. Kh1 Qf2 26. Rg1 Bxd5 27. Re4!. If immediately 24. ... Bxd5, White plays 25. Rd1!, when after 25. ... Rxg2+ 26. Kf1 gxh6, the moves 27. Rxh6 or 27. Rxd5 are not good enough, so White's best move is 27. Qxh6. But in any case, Black has a bishop and two pawns for the rook, giving him good chances for the win. It is understandable that Geller did not find these complex variations during the game.

Subsequent analysis has proved that 22. ... Rh8 was premature, and that it would have been better to play 22. ... Rc4 first. However, chess lovers would probably not agree. Moves like 22. ... Rh8 are hard to forget!

24. ...	**Rxg2+**
25. Kf1	**Qb3**
26. Ke1	**Qf3**
White resigns.	

Lesson Four

Pawn Attacks with Same-Side Castling

In this lesson we will give examples of attacks using pawns when the kings are castled on the same side. We will start with a position in which only one pawn takes part in the attack, and then we will move on to full-scale pawn attacks. Along the way, we will note useful general principles.

In the following examples, one or more pawns are used in the attack against the opponent's king for one of two purposes: (1) to weaken the position of the king, or (2) to open up lines for the attacker's pieces. Sometimes the pawn advance accomplishes both goals.

We are *not* going to consider here positions where pawns are used to create protected outpost squares for the pieces and do not play an active attacking role themselves (a very common situation). For example, in the Dutch Defense (1. d4 f5), a Black knight usually occupies the e4-square, protected by the f5-pawn. And in many variations of the Ruy Lopez (1. e4 e5 2. Nf3 Nc6 3. Bb5), a White knight often goes to f5, where it is supported by the e4-pawn and also sometimes by pawns on h3 and g4.

Attacking with one pawn

Creating a weakness

Diagram 155
Reti — Alekhine
Baden-Baden, 1925

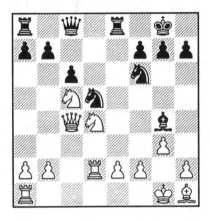

Position after White's 20th move

White controls the half open c-file on the queenside. If he could open it completely and occupy it with heavy pieces, he would gain a clear advantage. In addition, removing the c6-pawn takes away the supporter of the knight on d5, and provides more space for White's fianchettoed bishop, which is pointed toward the queenside.

How can White open the c-file?

The standard plan in cases like this is the pawn advance b2-b4-b5. If Black exchanges pawns on b5, then White's goal of opening the c-file would be reached. But if Black does not capture, White will take on c6, and Black will be left with a weak c6-pawn which will become a target. Black can delay the move b4-b5 by playing ... a7-a6, but then White plays a2-a4 with the idea of playing b4-b5 anyway. In chess literature, White's advance is known as the *minority attack,* where two pawns attack the opposing chain of three pawns.

What can Black do? Should he just wait passively for his opponent's queenside initiative to develop? Of course not! That means that he must make a plan on the other side of the board, because he does not have the option of attacking in the center. Black would accomplish nothing with a piece attack on the kingside because he does not have enough pieces there, and White's castled position is fairly strong.

The right idea for Black in this position is to weaken the position of White's king and then to attack it. Black plans h7-h5-h4-hxg3 in order to reduce the number of pawns sheltering the White king by exchanging. So, in this case the reason for advancing the rook's pawn is not to open up a file, but to weaken the opponent's kingside.

Even if Black achieves this goal, however, it is hard to see how he will benefit from it. We will follow Alekhine's play, and learn how to make use of such a weakness.

20. ...	h5!
21. b4	

We should also add that 21. e4 limits the bishop on h1 and does not give White anything real—for example, 21. ... Nb6 22. Qc3 Nbd7.

21. ...	a6
22. Rc1	

Necessary. After 22. a4 White could not immediately continue with b4-b5 because the a1-rook would be unprotected.

22. ...	h4
23. a4	hxg3
24. hxg3	Qc7

Diagram 156

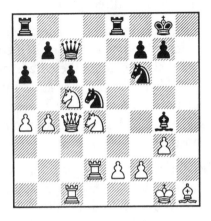

The pawn protection of the White king has been slightly weakened, but Black has no specific threats right now. It looks like he cannot even dream about making a successful attack. Thus, White pays attention only to his own plan. But in retrospect, we should say that 25. e4 was better.

| 25. b5 | axb5 |
| 26. axb5 | Re3! |

Diagram 157

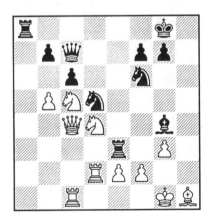

A brilliant move! The real attack on the king starts. Note that 27. fxe3 Qxg3+ 28. Bg2 Nxe3 loses for White.

27. Nf3

White needs to defend against ... Rxg3, but a better way to achieve this was 27. Bf3.

27. ...	**cxb5**
28. Qxb5	**Nc3**

Diagram 158

29. Qxb7

On 29. Qc4 Black could reply 29. ... Ra4. Now it is instructive to watch how Black continues the attack without queens.

29. ...	**Qxb7**

After 29. ... Nxe2+ White would have an extra defensive option (30. Rxe2 Qxb7 31. Rxe3), with chances for a successful defense.

30. Nxb7	**Nxe2+**

Diagram 159

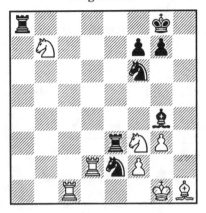

31. Kh2

On 31. Kf1 Black would play 31. ... Nxg3+ 32. fxg3 Bxf3 33. Bxf3 Rxf3+ 34. Kg2 and now not 34. ... Rxg3+ (because after 35. Kxg3 Ne4+ 36. Kf4 Nxd2 37. Nc5, Black has a bad knight), but instead 34. ... Raa3, for example: 35. Rd8+ Kh7 36. Rh1+ Kg6 37. Rh3 Rfb3, etc.

After 31. Rxe2 Rxe2 all the action would still be on one flank. But being the Exchange ahead in these kinds of positions makes it easier to win than having a queen against a rook and piece.

31. ...   Ne4!
32. Rc4

A great piece struggle is taking place. It is not good for White to play 32. fxe3 Nxd2, when Black wins the Exchange.

32. ...   Nxf2

If 32. ... Nxd2 then 33. Nxd2, and Black's rook and bishop are under attack— for example, 33. ... Rd3 34. Nc5.

32. Bg2

Black has won a pawn. But since the action is taking place on only one side of the board, trying to win by simplifying the position is rather problematic. Many endgames like this end as a draw, so Black continues to attack.

Diagram 160

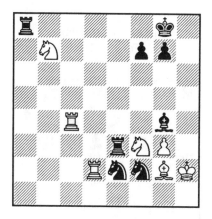

33. ...   Be6!

Black frees the g4-square for the knight with gain of tempo. The rest is easy to understand.

34. Rcc2 Ng4+ 35. Kh3 Ne5+ 36. Kh2 Rxf3! 37. Rxe2 Ng4+ 38. Kh3 Ne3+ 39. Kh2 Nxc2 40. Bxf3 Nd4

Diagram 161

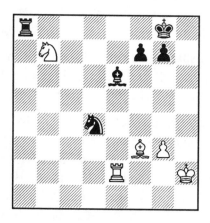

White resigns, because after 41. Re3 Nxf3+ 42. Rxf3 Bd5, Black wins a piece.

Opening a file

Diagram 162
Lasker — Capablanca
Moscow, 1935

Position after Black's 18th move

White's position is better. All of his pieces are on good squares. At the same time Black suffers from a misplaced queen on a5 and a bishop on d7 that does not have much of a future. After the eventual exchange of dark-squared bishops, the position of Black's king will be seriously weakened.

This situation suggests a kingside attack. White can transfer his queen and a rook to the kingside by using the e-file, after which he will have all of his pieces participating in the attack.

We should also point out that Black does not have the possibility of a counter-attack on either the queenside or the center. That is why White does not hurry with a piece attack, but instead starts by moving his rook's pawn. By a similar pawn advance in the previous example, Alekhine weakened the position of his opponent's king, but the open file was not a factor in the struggle. In this case, by moving the rook's pawn forward, White not only weakens the position of the Black king but also prepares to use the open file in the attack.

19. h4!   **Qd8**

It is bad to play 19. ... h5, because of 20. Bxg6 fxg6 21. Qxg6
Re7 22. Rd3, with a winning attack for White. Black moves his
queen to the defense, because the threat is 20. h5 followed by
an exchange of pawns and the sacrifice of the bishop on g6. This
threat could have been prevented by 19. ... f5, but in that case
Black's position would further deteriorate because of the weak
pawn on e6.

20. h5	**Qg5**
21. Bxg7	**Kxg7**
22. Re5	**Qe7**

Diagram 163

If 22. ... f5 White has no reason to exchange pawns because
after 23. hxg6 hxg6 Black would control the h-file. It is better
to sacrifice the h5-pawn by playing 22. Bc4 Qxh5 23. Rde1.
This threatens 24. Qb3, after which White would win back the
pawn and keep his positional advantage because the e-file will
be in his hands, and the position of the Black king will remain
unsafe.

23. Rde1   **Rg8**

Preparing ... Kf8.

24. Qc1

| 24. ... | Rad8 |

On 24. ... Kf8 White continues 25. Qh6+ Rg7 26. R1e3 and all of White's pieces are aimed at Black's kingside.

25. R1e3

Diagram 164

| 25. ... | Bc8 |

Both now and on the next move, ... f7-f6, while deserving consideration, would not ease the defense. For example: 25. ... f6 26. Ra5 a6 27. hxg6 hxg6 28. Rg3, creating further weaknesses.

| **26. Rh3** | **Kf8** |

Black can offer more resistance with 26. ... Rh8.

| **27. Qh6+** | **Rg7** |
| **28. hxg6** | **hxg6** |

Diagram 165

29. Bxg6!

Because Black's castled position has been weakened by the exchange of pawns, it can now be destroyed by a simple combination. Since 29. ... fxg6 loses to 30. Qh8+ and 31. Rf3+, Black has lost a pawn and still has the worse position.

29. ...	**Qf6**
30. Rg5!	

There is no defense against 31. Rf3. Black could set a trap by playing 30. ... Rd5, because after 31. Rf3 Qxf3! 32. gxf3 Rxg5+!, Black wins. However, after 31. Qh8+ Ke7 32. Rxd5 cxd5 (in case of 32. ... exd5 33. Qxc8 the White rook would occupy the e-file) 33. Qxc8 Qxg6 34. Qc7+, White's victory is near.

30. ...	**Ke7**
31. Rf3	**Qxf3**
32. gxf3	

Diagram 166

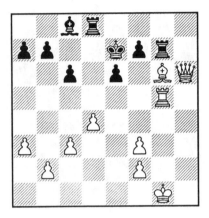

White's advantage is now decisive, and he went on to win.

Activating every piece

Diagram 167
Botvinnik — Vidmar
Nottingham, 1936

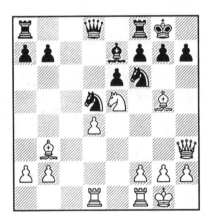

Position after Black's 16th move

Black's position seems fairly safe. White's queen, knight and bishops can operate on the kingside, but Black's kingside pawn formation is strong. It looks like White can't break through.

White has an isolated d-pawn, and if the game is simplified White will have to worry about protecting it. The most logical plan for White in such a position is a kingside attack. However, by using only the pieces currently in play it will be difficult to mount a successful assault. White's rooks currently do not play an active role, so he should think about activating them. Botvinnik finds the idea of opening the f-file.

17. f4!   Rc8

On 17. ... g6, trying to stop the breakthrough f4-f5, White will win the Exchange after 18. Bh6 Re8 19. Ba4, and 17. ... Ne4 18. Bc2 also gives White the advantage.

Unable to stop f4-f5, Black makes a developing move and prevents a future Bc2.

18. f5   exf5

Also better for White is 18. ... Qd6 19. fxe6, or 18. ... Ne4 19. Bxe7 Qxe7 20. Rfe1.

19. Rxf5   Qd6

Diagram 168

A tactical oversight. However, Black's position is already difficult. White threatened to strengthen the attack with 20. Rdf1, with all his pieces joining the attack.

20. Nxf7!	**Rxf7**
21. Bxf6	**Bxf6**

Or 21. ... Nxf6 22. Rxf6 Bxf6 23. Qxc8+.

Diagram 169

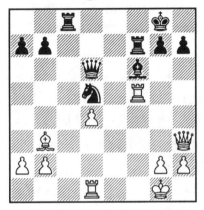

22. Rxd5	**Qc6**
23. Rd6	**Qe8**
24. Rd7	**Black resigns.**

Advancing prematurely

Diagram 170
Brinkman — Bogolyubov
Triberg, 1921

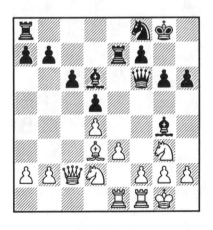

Position after Black's 15th move

16. f4?

This is a serious mistake. White's attack after this move is an illusion, but the weakness on e3 is real.

16. ...	**Rae8**
17. f5	**g5**
18. Kf2	

This is the best defense, but it is still not good enough. A beautiful mating combination follows.

Diagram 171

18. ...	**Rxe3!!**
19. Rxe3	**Rxe3**
20. Kxe3	**Bf4+**
21. Rxf4	

Or 21. Kf2 Qxd4+ 22. Ke1 Bxg3+ 23. hxg3 Qe3+, with checkmate.

21. ...	**gxf4+**
22. Kxf4	

Hopeless for White is 22. Kf2 Qxd4+ 23. Kf1 fxg3 24. hxg3 Qe3+.

Diagram 172

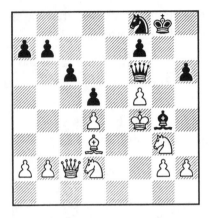

22. ...	Qg5+
23. Ke5	Ng6+
24. Kd6	Qe7 mate.

We have already mentioned that attacking with the knight's pawn weakens one's own position and runs a high risk of counterattack. The knight pawn usually attacks together with the rook pawn or the bishop pawn. The following game illustrates such an attack.

Wing thrust vs. central counterplay

Diagram 173
Unzicker — Reshevsky
International Tournament, 1958

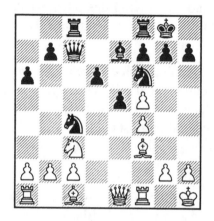

Position after Black's 15th move

First let's try to determine the character of the position. Is it open or closed? This kind of evaluation here can be only approximate.

For now there are no open files, but there are also no pawn chains, which would give the game more of a closed character. In our opinion this position should not be classified as truly open, but it is more open than closed.

What plan should White adopt? On which side of the board can he become active? Can he be active on the queenside? No, because Black is stronger on this part of the board.

Who stands better in the center? White currently controls the central squares e4 and d5, but we also have to consider that Black has two center pawns (a precondition for a possible attack in the center).

The right conclusion is that White should play on the kingside. It is rather difficult to prepare a piece attack there, but

White has a majority of pawns on the kingside, which suggests a pawn attack.

16. g4

White starts a pawn attack on the kingside with the help of the g-pawn. Although moving this pawn weakens the position of the White king, in the given situation Black is not able to exploit this weakening.

White's basic plan is to play 17. g5, followed by moving his knight to the central square d5. Occupying this strong square stops Black's chances of seizing the initiative in the center. After occupying the central outpost on d5, White would continue the pawn attack on the kingside so as to open lines for a piece attack.

16. ...   e4

Since it is not possible to stop g4-g5, Reshevsky strikes in the center, sacrificing a pawn. While Black's plan does not succeed in this particular game, we must say that his idea is logical and correct. It fails simply because White was better and played correctly.

17. Nxe4   Rfe8

Black wants to advance his d-pawn so he will have open files and diagonals for counterplay.

18. Nxf6+   Bxf6
19. Qf2   Bxb2

Diagram 174

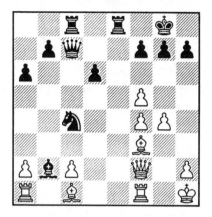

This does not win back the sacrificed pawn, but if Black plays differently he would simply be a pawn down—for example, 19. ... b5 20. c3, and White threatens to continue the attack with 21. g5.

20. Bxb2	**Nxb2**
21. Rab1	**Na4**

It is not possible to take the pawn on c2 because of 22. Rxb2.

22. Rxb7

Diagram 175

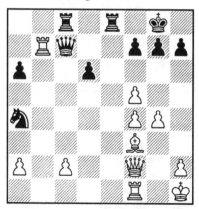

22. ...	**Qc4**

Again taking the c2-pawn is not good: 22. ... Qxc2 23. Qxc2 Rxc2 24. Bd5. Black moves the queen to c4 so that the White bishop cannot occupy d5.

23. Qg2   Nc3

Now the knight also guards the d5-square. White's obvious threats are defended against; however, he can continue the attack on the kingside (which was interrupted by Black's counterattack in the center).

24. g5

The threat is to open lines with 25. g6. These would be very dangerous for Black because of the White queen on the g-file and the White rook on the 7th rank. That is why with his next move Black tries to exchange this active rook.

24. ...   Rb8
25. Rd7

Diagram 176

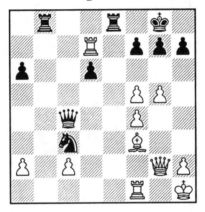

25. ...   Rb1

Reshevsky probably overlooked that this quickly leads to the worse position because of the following combination.

Of course, it was much better to continue hunting the rook with 25. ... Rbd8, when White would reply 26. Ra7. White would still have the advantage, but the win would be a long way off.

Notice also that 25. ... Qxf4 could be answered by 26. g6. This is stronger than 26. Bd5, after which the sacrifice 26. ... Nxd5 is possible.

26. Rxb1   Nxb1
27. Qe2!!

An unexpected tactical blow!

27. ...   Qc8

The endgame after 27. ... Qxe2 28. Bxe2 would be lost for Black, because he is a pawn down in a bad position.

28. Rc7!

Diagram 177

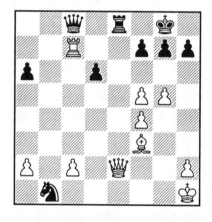

Another bad surprise for Black.

28. ...   Qd8
29. Qc4   d5

Black is lost: **30. Bxd5 Nd2 31. Qc6 Rf8 32. Rxf7 Rxf7 33. g6 hxg6 34. fxg6 Kf8 35. gxf7 Ne4 36. Qe8+ Black resigns.**

Attacking with multiple pawns

Now let's consider positions in which the attack on the king is made by using all the kingside pawns.

Space advantage

Diagram 178
Gereban — Smyslov
Moscow, 1949

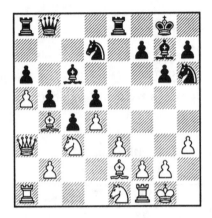

Position after White's 21st move

Black has a majority of pawns on the queenside, and White must blockade them because otherwise they will become a serious threat. The need to maintain this blockade prevents White from seeking active play, which gives Black the advantage. In addition, Black's pieces have greater maneuverability.

Considering the fact that the center is not open and the position has a closed character, Smyslov decided to start a pawn advance on the kingside, with the idea of opening the files for his pieces and weakening the position of the White king.

21. ...	f5
22. Nc2	

On 22. Bd6 Black could answer 22. ... Qd8 and 23. ... Bf8.

22. ...	Nf7

The immediate 22. ... f4 is not possible because of 23. Bd6. But Black has no need to hurry. First of all he improves the position of his pieces.

23. Be7

White clears the b4-square for his knight, intending to put pressure on the d5-pawn. By exchanging bishops, Black takes away possible counterplay.

23. ...	Bf6
24. Bxf6	Nxf6

Diagram 179

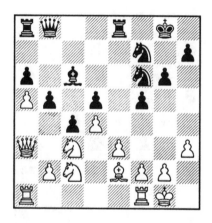

25. Nb4

Ineffective would be 25. Qc5 because after 25. ... Bb7 White cannot increase the pressure on d5. For example: 26. Nb4 Nd7 and the queen is trapped, or 26. Bf3 Ng5 27. Bxd5 and White loses material after 27. ... Nxd5 28. Nxd5 Ne4 29. Ne7+ Kf7 30. Nc6 Nxc5 31. Nxb8 Nb3.

25. ...	Bb7
26. Bf3	Qd8

Now the d-pawn is strongly protected. But before continuing with the pawn attack on the kingside, Black improves the positions of his pieces.

27. g3

This move weakens White's castled position, but he wants to reposition the bishop to g2 where it will put some pressure on the d5-pawn. In a couple of moves Black will prepare ... f5-f4, which has become more difficult to play after g2-g3. So we cannot really say that 27. g3 helps Black to open files for an attack.

27. ...	Ng5
28. Bg2	Nge4
29. Nxe4	Nxe4
30. Nc2	

Diagram 180

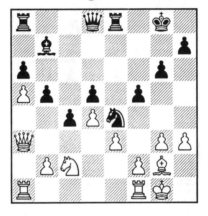

White cannot solve his problems by exchanging his bishop for the strong, centralized knight, because after 30. Bxe4 fxe4 his kingside is bare.

Black has finished improving the placement of his pieces, and is ready to continue advancing his pawns. That is why White brings the knight over for defense. White probably also thought that the weakened e5-square would be good to occupy with a knight.

| 30. ... | g5 |
| 31. Ne1 | Qf6 |

Black preferred not to win the Exchange with 31. ... Nd2 because White could then establish his knight on e5, and would have drawing chances.

32. Nf3

Diagram 181

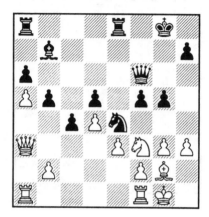

The White knight is moving toward e5. Black is ready with the first breakthrough on the kingside.

32. ...	f4
33. exf4	

After the immediate 33. g4, then 33. ... Rf8, with the idea of opening the f-file, is strong.

33. ...	gxf4
34. g4	

White prevents the opening of a file on the kingside for the moment, but Black has another way to open lines.

34. ...   Rad8

Black plans a "rook lift" on the kingside with ... Rd6-h6.

35. Rfe1	h5
36. Ne5	

Now the h-file will be open, but 36. gxh5 would not help because Black would then attack on the g-file.

36. ...	hxg4
37. hxg4	Qh4
38. Qf3	

Diagram 182

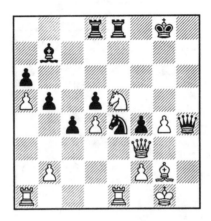

| 38. ... | Rd6 |

From here the rook can go to h6. Black wants his other rook on f8 so he can play ... Ng5 and ... f4-f3. So he first takes the square g6 under control to prevent a fork with Ng6.

39. Rad1

On 39. Qxf4, Black answers with 39. ... Rf8 40. Qe3 Rxf2.

| 39. ... | Rf8 |
| 40. Bf1 | |

White already has no useful moves.

| 40. ... | Rh6 |
| 41. Bg2 | |

On 41. Qg2 f3 42. Nxf3 Rxf3 wins.

Diagram 183

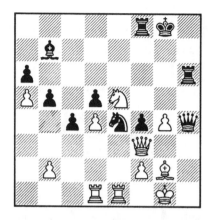

| 41. ... | b4 |

Black could have won by playing 41. ... Qh2+ 42. Kf1 Ng3+ 43. fxg3 fxg3, but he is in no hurry because White is completely helpless.

| 42. Kf1 | Ng5 |
| 43. Qe2 | f3 |

Diagram 184

Winning a piece. White still struggled for quite a few moves:
44. Nxf3 Nxf3 45. Bxf3 Rhf6 46. Kg2 Rxf3 47. Qxf3 Rxf3 48. Kxf3 Bc6 49. Re5 c3 50. bxc3 bxc3 51. Rc1 Qh3+ 52. Kf4

**Bd7 53. Re3 Qxg4+ 54. Ke5 Qe6+ 55. Kf4 Qf5+ 56. Kg3 c2
White resigns.**

The next example shows a type of pawn attack which is very
useful to know because it occurs frequently.

Slow buildup

**Diagram 185
Reti — Carls
Baden-Baden, 1925**

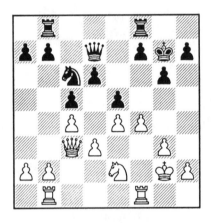

Position after Black's 20th move

21. f5!

In this situation it would not be good to open the f-file because
after 21. fxe5 dxe5 White exposes his pawn weakness at d3 and
cannot efficiently use the newly-opened f-file.

21. ...   f6

The threat was f5-f6+ followed by Qc3-d2-h6. It would not
be good to play 21. ... gxf5?, because after 22. Rxf5 Black's king
position would be very weak. Now White will play Ne2-c3-d5,
followed by Rf2 and Rbf1. The goal of this plan is to make Black
play ... g6-g5, giving White the means to open the h-file for the
decisive attack.

| 22. Qd2 | g5 |

Black should not have played this move so quickly; he is eager to close the position on the kingside so he can start a queenside counterattack. But Reti brilliantly refutes Black's plan.

| 23. g4 | b5 |
| 24. h4 | |

White's plan is to open the h-file and invade the opponent's camp with heavy pieces.

24. ...	h6
25. Rh1	bxc4
26. dxc4	Nd4
27. Nc3	Rh8
28. Rh3!	

Diagram 186

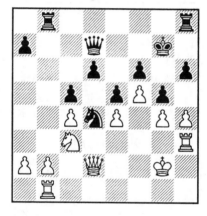

This is a good example of how to fight for an open file. White is not in a hurry to open the h-file. He makes use of his space advantage by taking the time to double rooks before opening the file.

28. ...	Rbg8
29. Rbh1	Qd8
30. Nd5	gxh4

This move exposes the weakness of the h6-pawn. But left unhindered, White would increase the pressure with moves like Kf1 and Qh2, preparing hxg5.

Diagram 187

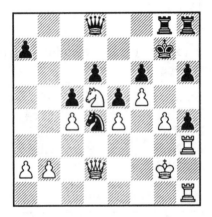

31. Rxh4	Kf7
32. Kf2!	Qf8
33. Rxh6	Rxh6
34. Rxh6	Qg7
35. Qa5!	**Black resigns.**

Diagram 188

It is important to note that White was able to prepare his attack slowly and calmly because the position was closed and stable.

When the kings are castled on the same side, advancing the pawns in front of one's own king must not be rushed. This caution is easy to understand—preparation is required before you can open files leading to your own king. But if the kings have castled in different directions, then the pawn attack can occur very rapidly, as we will see in lesson five.

Opening files

Diagram 189
Alekhine — Astalosh
Kecskemet, 1927

Position after Black's 26th move

In this example, two out of the three white kingside pawns will take part in the attack. In evaluating this position, it's important to notice White's advantage in the location of his forces. His pieces have a lot of room to maneuver. Since the position on both the queenside and in the center has a closed character, White starts an attack on the kingside in which pawns play a big role.

If Black could take direct action in the center, his bishop pair might become a factor. But weakening the position of the White king (by advancing the kingside pawns) is not significant here because Black does not have any such counterplay.

27. h4!

White plans to move his bishop to b1 and then to create mate threats on the b1-h7 diagonal. The pawn move discourages potential defense by ... g7-g6, to which White can now answer h4-h5.

27. ...	Raa8
28. Bb1	h5

The threat was 29. Qc2 g6 30. h5. Black cannot play ... f7-f5 either now or on the next move because it would create a permanent weakness on e6.

29. Qf3	g6

Diagram 190

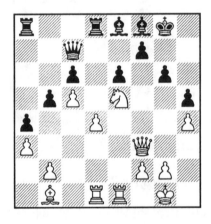

30. g4!

The defensive wall in front of the Black king starts to crack.

30. ...	hxg4
31. Qxg4	Bg7
32. Ba2	

With this move White stops Black from moving the f-pawn. However, 32. h5 was even better.

32. ...	b4

Black sacrifices a pawn in return for some initiative—for example, 33. axb4 a3 34. bxa3 Rxa3. Of course White declines this gift.

| 33. Bc4 | bxa3 |
| 34. bxa3 | Qa5 |

Diagram 191

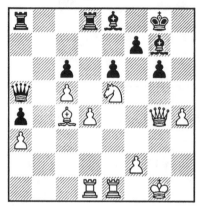

Now White can't continue with the immediate 35. Nxg6 because of 35. ... Rxd4. The same counterattack would follow after 35. h5 gxh5 36. Qxh5.

| **35. Qe4** | **Qc7** |

On 35. ... Qc3 White would answer 36. Re3. Black probably moved his queen because he feared 36. Nxg6; however, it would be better to play 35. ... Rab8 because then after 36. Nxg6 Black could play 36. ... Rxd4. (Bad is 36. ... fxg6 in view of 37. Qxe6+ Kh7 38. Qg8+ Kh6 39. Re7.) After 35. ... Rab8 White would probably continue 36. Re3.

| **36. Qf4** | |

After the immediate 36. h5, Black answers with 36. ... g5, which is why by moving his queen White prepares this breakthrough. Now 36. ... Qe7 is bad because of 37. Nxg6 fxg6 38. Rxe6.

| **36. ...** | **Rab8** |
| **37. h5!** | |

Diagram 192

This opens the g-file for White's rooks.

37. ...	gxh5
38. Kh1	Rb7
39. Rg1	Qe7
40. Rxg7+	Kxg7
41. Rg1+	Kh7

Diagram 193

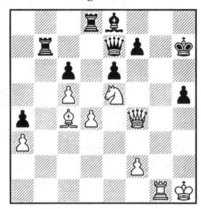

42. Nxf7!

After this **Black resigns** because 42. ... Qxf7 43. Bd3+ loses the queen while White's attack will still continue: 43. ... Qg6 44. Qf8!.

The next example shows the danger of moving pawns in front of your own king without concern for counterattack.

Queenside counterplay

Diagram 194
Bisguier — Petrosian
New York, 1954

Position after Black's 17th move

Black's queenside attack has been a success so far, and at the same time White does not yet have an attack in the center or on the kingside. How should White continue the struggle? What plan should he choose?

If we look carefully at the position, our attention will be drawn to the move g3-g4, because White's best chances are on the kingside. White cannot "stand still," since that means gradually giving away important squares to his opponent. However, we think that after 18. g4 Nd7 19. g5 Nc5 20. h4 Rd8, Black's chances are better because it is difficult for White to make progress on the kingside, while Black could start active operations on the queenside. But after 18. g4, the struggle would be very sharp.

18. Rab1

White moves the rook so that after 18. ... a3 he can play 19. Ba1, keeping the bishop on the long diagonal. However, there is no reason for Black to close the queenside with ... a4-a3 if it does not bring an immediate advantage, since all his chances lie in creating an initiative on the queenside. After 18. g4 a3 19. Bc1, White would not have to worry about the queenside and could then turn his full attention to kingside activity.

So 18. Rb1 is ineffective: White prevents ... a4-a3, a move that Black would not play anyway, and White gives away the open a-file to his opponent, who will use it to invade the second rank.

18. ...	**axb3**
19. axb3	**Ra2**

Black is happy with the recent changes in the position.

20. g4	**Nd7**
21. g5	**Re8**

This move frees f8 for the bishop.

22. Kh1

Diagram 195

It would be better to play 22. h4 if White decided to attack the king. However, Black's rook occupies such a strong position on a2 that White's chances for a successful pawn attack are small. How can White evict the rook from a2? He can play 22. Nf3 Nc5 23. Qc2, preparing 24. Ra1, but after 23. ... Bb7 24. Ra1 R8a8 Black is still better.

22. ...	Nc5
23. h4	Qd8

Black wants to improve his position by playing ... e6-e5 and controlling d4. He moves his queen so that White will not play Nd5 with tempo. If White continues with 24. f5, he loses control over the important square e5.

24. Rf3	Bf8
25. Rg3	e5!

Diagram 196

Black begins active operations in the center — an effective antidote to White's pawn advance on the kingside.

26. f5	Nd4
27. Qf1	

If 27. Bxd4 exd4 28. Nd5, then 28. ... Bxf5, and 27. Qd1 would be followed by 27. ... Nd3.

27. ...	Ndxb3
28. Nxb3	Nxb3
29. Qe1	Nc5!

Diagram 197

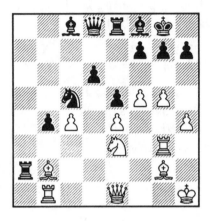

Black sacrifices a pawn to achieve a decisive positional advantage.

30. Qxb4	Bb7
31. Nd5	Ra4
32. Qd2	

On 32. Qc3 good is 32. ... Ba6 33. Ne3 Qb8, followed by 34. ... Rb4.

32. ...	Bxd5

The simplest because White cannot escape the pin on the b-file without losing material.

33. Qxd5	Rb4
34. Bf3	Qa8
35. Qd2	Qb7
36. Rg2	Rb8

Diagram 198

37. Bd1

The threat was 37. ... Na4. A few more moves were played:
**37. ... Qxe4 38. Bc2 Qxc4 39. g6 Rxb2 40. gxh7+ Kh8
41. Rbg1 Qxh4+ 42. Rh2 Qf4 White resigns.**

White's troubles in this game arose because of the weakening
of his king's castled position and because his pieces were not
well placed for active play.

Transition to the endgame

Diagram 199
Riumin — Kan
Moscow, 1936

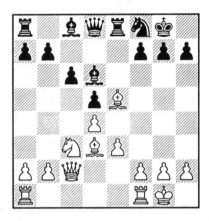

Position after Black's 13th move

**14. f4! f6 15. Bxd6 Qxd6 16. Rf3 Be6 17. Kh1 Re7
18. Rg1 Rae8 19. g4 Bf7 20. Qf2 Kh8**

Diagram 200

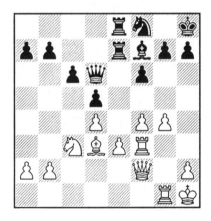

21. h4

Since Black has no strong counterplay in the center, White can launch a successful pawn storm. This position differs from the Brinkman—Bogolyubov game in Lesson Four because White's e3-pawn is well protected. Black has no way to increase the pressure, so White can launch a successful pawn storm.

21. ... a6 22. f5 c5 23. Ne2 cxd4 24. exd4 Qb4 25. Nf4 Re1 26. Rfg3 Rxg1+ 27. Rxg1 Qe7 28. g5 fxg5 29. hxg5

Diagram 201

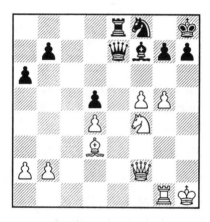

Black's central counterplay comes too late. White's attack is well under way and can continue even without queens on the board.

29. ... Qe3 30. Qxe3 Rxe3 31. Kg2 Be8 32. Kf2 Re7 33. Rc1 Bc6 34. Kf3 Rf7 35. Kg4 Rc7

Diagram 202

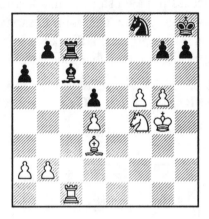

The result of the attack is "only" a better ending, with more space and better pieces. Now comes another stage of the game — converting this advantage into victory.

36. Ne6   Nxe6

It would have been better to play 36. ... Rc8 here.

37. fxe6 Kg8 38. Kf5 Kf8 39. Ke5 g6 40. Kd6 Re7 41. Bxa6 Ke8 42. Bd3 Black resigns.

Exercises

1

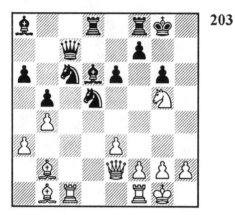

203

White to move

2

204

Black to move

3

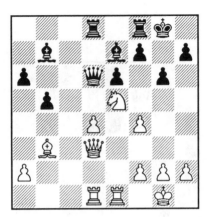

205

White to move

4

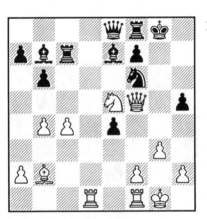

206

White to move

5

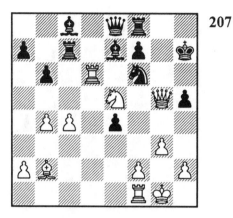

207

White to move

6

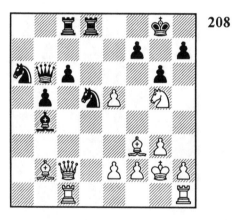

208

White to move

7

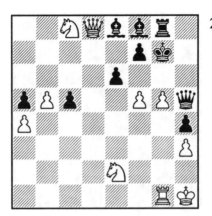

209

White to move

8

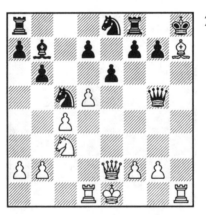

210

White to move

9

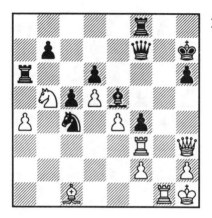

211

White to move

10

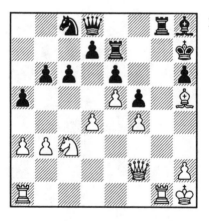

212

White to move

11

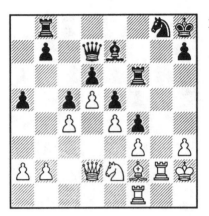

213

Black to move

12

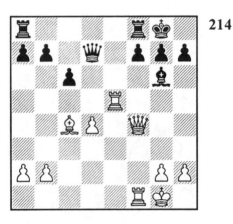

214

White to move

Solutions

1. *Marshall — Wolf, Nuremberg, 1906.* White has everything prepared for an attack on the Black king. His bishops on b2 and b1 and the knight at g5 are active, and bringing the queen into play will make the attack unstoppable. This example supports our general rule that it is important to involve as many pieces as possible in the attack. **1. Qh5! f6** (of course not 1. ... gxh5 2. Bh7 mate) **2. Bxg6 Rd7 3. Nxe6 Black resigns.**

2. *Levitsky — Marshall, Breslau, 1912.* Black has a material advantage, but two of his pieces are under attack. Still, Marshall's heavy pieces can use the half-open files to launch a winning attack. Black makes use of several pins to create a combination. **1. ... Qg3!.** After this White can only resign — he has no saving moves. For example, 2. hxg3 Ne2 mate or 2. fxg3 Ne2+ 3. Kh1 Rxf1 mate, and after 2. Qxg3 Ne2+ 3. Kh1 Nxg3+ 4. Kg1 Nxf1 5. gxh3 Nd2 Black wins easily.

3. *Alekhine — Seleznyev, Bad Pistyan, 1922.* This is a fragment from the game analysis. Here White could have unleashed **1. Nxg6! hxg6 2. Rxe6!** (to open more files) **2. ... fxe6 3. Qxg6+ Kh8 4. Bc2**, followed by mate in a few moves—for example, **4. ... Rf5 5. Rd3**, etc.

4. *Lerner — Razuvayev, Frunze, 1979.* **1. Rd6!.** By means of a combination, White brings his rook into the attack. The preconditions for an attack are clear: Black's king is open, the bishop on b2 is ready for action on the long diagonal, the queen is ready to make threats, and the knight on e5 is well placed. White intends to answer 1. ... Bxd6 with 2. Ng4! when Black's weakness on the long diagonal, especially on f6, will be fatal. **1. ... Bc8 2. Qg5+ Kh7.** Now go to position number 5.

5. *Lerner — Razuvayev, Frunze, 1979.* Continued from the previous position (after 1. Rd6! Bc8 2. Qg5+ Kh7). **3. Nd7!.** This is a wonderful move of great artistic merit since the knight can be captured four ways. If now 3. ... Bxd7 4. Rxf6 Bxf6 5. Bxf6, and now the only defense to Qg7 mate is 5. ... Rg8, which allows 6. Qxh5 mate. And 3. ... Rxd7 leads to the same predicament, while 3. ... Nxd7 4. Qg7 is mate. That leaves only **3. ... Qxd7**. Now 4. Rxf6 fails to 4. ... Bxf6 5. Bxf6 Qg4!, but the game concluded after **4. Rxd7 Bxd7 5. Bxf6 Bxf6 6. Qxf6 Rxc4 7. Qe7 Black resigns**.

6. *Ivanchuk — Yudasin, Riga, 1991.* Black has completely taken over the queenside; however, there are no easy targets left there. Black's pieces are misplaced and cannot aid his lonely king, who can only watch as lines open up and the enemy invades. **1. e6 fxe6 2. Qe4** and **Black resigns** because he cannot defend against White's threats.

7. *Ivanchuk — Kasparov, Linares, 1991.* White's advanced pawns, together with the disharmony in Black's position, play an important role in the attack. **1. Rg4!** This stops Black's queen from making a counterattack. **1. ... exf5 2. Nf4 Qh8**. Now both king and queen are trapped. **3. Qf6+ Kh7 4. Rxh4+** and mate next move, so **Black resigns**.

8. *Speelman — Kudrin, Hastings, 1983-4.* White has an open h-file, with his rook opposing Black's king. A couple of elegant preparatory moves make the position ready for a standard but beautiful combination: **1. Bc2+ Kg8 2. Rh5 Qf4 3. g3 Qf6 4. Bh7+ Kh8 5. Bg6+** and **Black resigns** because of 5. ... Kg8 6. Rh8+!! Kxh8 7. Qh5+ Kg8 (the bishop on g6 interferes with the queen's defense of h6) 8. Qh7 **mate**.

9. *Kramnik — Kasparov, Novgorod, 1997.* **1. Nc7!**. The knight joins the attack, and it can't be taken. (If 1. ... Qxc7? 2. Qxh6+ Kxh6 3. Rh3 checkmate!) The Black queen is overworked. Kramnik remarked: "Back in my childhood I was taught that such a motif is called *overloading*." **1. ... Rxa4 2. Bxf4 Black resigns**, because after 2. ... Bxf4 3. Ne6, Black loses in all lines — not surprising, with two Black pieces "missing in action" far off on the queenside. For example, if Black tries 3. ... Rg8, then 4. Rxg8 Qxg8 (or 4. ... Kxg8 5. Rxf4 with a rapid mate) 5. Qf5+ Kh8 6. Qf6+ Kh7 7. Nf8+, winning the queen.

10. *Kasparov — Yusupov, USSR Championship, 1981.* Black's knight on c8 is temporarily out of the game, and Black's extra pawn will mean little if White develops a kingside attack. **1. Ne4!** fxe4 (or else White will play Nf6) **2. f5!**. (Threatening to trap the rook with f5-f6, but Black cannot take the pawn because of 3. Qxf5+, followed by mate.) **2. ... Rg5 3. Rxg5 hxg5 4. f6** and White is winning. The remaining moves were **4. ... Kh6 5. fxe7 Qxe7 6. Bf7 d6 7. Rf1 g4 8. Bxe6 Qxe6 9. Qh4+** and **Black lost on time**.

11. *Averbakh — Kotov, Zurich, 1953.* **1. ... Qxh3+!!**. Sacrificing the queen for a pawn is quite rare in practice. Now after this thunderbolt, the king must make a dangerous journey while under fire from all Black's pieces. At the same time White's entire army is cut off by the wall of pawns and cannot rescue its king. **2. Kxh3 Rh6+ 3. Kg4 Nf6+ 4. Kf5**. Here Black was so excited by his queen sacrifice that he played **4. ... Nd7** and went on to win, missing **4. ... Ng4!**, which would have been immediately conclusive.

12. *Bogolyubov, Reti, and Spielmann — Englund, Jakobson, Nikholm, and Olson, Consultation game, Stockholm, 1919.* **1. h4!**. White has a very active position with pressure against f7. By moving his h-pawn he intends to drive the Black bishop away from defending the critical square. **1. ... Bc2.** (Other continuations were no better: 1. ... Rae8 2. h5 Bc2 3. Qxf7+ Rxf7 4. Rxf7 Qxd4+ 5. Rf2+ Qxc4 6. Rxe8 mate, or 2. ... Rxe5 3. dxe5 Bxh5 4. e6 Qe7 5. Qe5.) **2. Qe3 Rad8** (on 2. ... Rae8 follows 3. Rxf7 Rxf7 4. Rxe8+) **3. Rxf7 Rxf7 4. Re7 Qc8 5. Rxf7 Kh8 6. Rxg7!**. The final blow, exposing the king. **Black resigns** since 6. ... Kxg7 7. Qe7+ is mate in two.

Part III:

Attacks with Opposite-Side Castling

Lesson Five

Attacks with Opposite-Side Castling

When the kings are castled on opposite sides of the board, a very sharp and complex battle often arises. Both sides try to develop a swift attack, and whoever outraces the opponent usually obtains the advantage. In such attacks, the rapid advance of pawns often plays an important role. Pawn exchanges can clear a path for the attacking forces, and the advance of attacking pawns can also create weak points that the attacker can exploit.

But simply moving pawns toward the enemy king does not necessarily create favorable attacking conditions. Castling on opposite sides creates a dynamic situation with two fighting fronts in which the most significant factors are (1) time, (2) the initiative, and (3) conformity to general principles of positional play. Also very important are (4) controlling the center, (5) superior development, and (6) having an advantage in attacking force near the enemy king. These six factors are the best way to evaluate the attacking chances for each side.

There are many classical examples of attacks with the kings on opposite flanks. Paul Morphy's games, for example, contain many instructive examples.

Superior mobility and coordination

Diagram 215
Bird — Morphy
London, 1858

1. e4 e5 2. Nf3 d6 3. d4 f5 4. Nc3 fxe4 5. Nxe4 d5 6. Ng3 e4 7. Ne5 Nf6 8. Bg5 Bd6 9. Nh5 0-0 10. Qd2 Qe8 11. g4 Nxg4 12. Nxg4 Qxh5 13. Ne5 Nc6 14. Be2 Qh3 15. Nxc6 bxc6 16. Be3 Rb8 17. 0-0-0

Some commentators have remarked at this point that Black's win is just a "matter of technique." It's true that White's position is indefensible: Not only is he a pawn down, but he also has weak pawns on the kingside, and the open b-file provides Black with splendid attacking chances. The open g-file is meaningless because Black has more space on the kingside as well. Nevertheless, Black's next two moves, which at first seem totally irrational, are not easy to find.

17. ...	**Rxf2!?**
18. Bxf2	**Qa3!!**

This transfer of the queen is made possible by Black's rook on the b-file. Now of course it would be a blunder to play 19. bxa3? Bxa3 mate.

Diagram 216

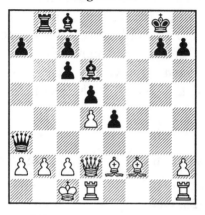

19. c3	Qxa2

On the basis of material alone, one would now declare White the winner, but this would be a mistake. In this position the important action is on the queenside, where the coordinated activity of Black's remaining forces matters more than White's overall advantage in material. White's king cannot escape, and his extra rook cannot protect him.

20. b4	Qa1+
21. Kc2	Qa4+

Diagram 217

22. Kb2?

This is the critical moment of the combination. White fails to
find the correct square for his king, and loses by force. Instead
22. Kc1 would have given Black a choice between drawing with
repeated queen checks and maintaining the initiative with
22. ... a5!, to which we give just one sample continuation:
23. Bg3 axb4 24. Bxd6 Qa1+ 25. Kc2 b3 mate!

22. ...	**Bxb4**
23. cxb4	**Rxb4+**

Now the pursuit of the White king begins to bear fruit.

24. Qxb4	**Qxb4+**
25. Kc2	**e3**
26. Bxe3	**Bf5+**
27. Rd3	**Qc4+**

The same move would have followed 27. Bd3.

28. Kd2	**Qa2+**
29. Kd1	**Qb1+**

and **Black won** after taking the rook on h1.

No counterplay

Diagram 218
Capablanca — Janowsky
St. Petersburg, 1914

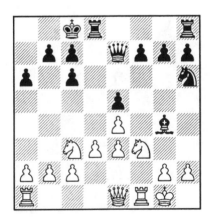

Position after Black's 10th move

The Black king is surrounded by many pawns. However, the pawns on a6 and c6 give White the possibility of creating a pawn attack by playing b4, a4 and b5 after proper preparation. Neither side has any play on the kingside or in the center.

11. Rab1

This begins the attack. White prepares b2-b4.

11. ...   f6

Black wants to use f7 to bring his knight to the defense, especially since the knight on h6 is not doing anything useful. Trying to stop b2-b4 with 11. ... c5 does not work because White will continue 12. Nd5 and 13. b4. Likewise after 11. ... a5, White can simply prepare with 12. a3.

12. b4	**Nf7**
13. a4	**Bxf3**

There is no reason to make this exchange, but Black does not know what to do since he has no targets for counterplay.

14. Rxf3   b6

Diagram 219

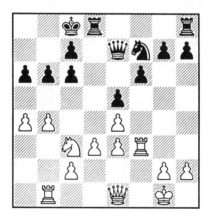

Black plans to arrange his pawns to prevent the opening of files after b5. If 14. ... b5 then 15. Ne2, intending to transfer the knight to b3. White's positional advantage is clear.

15. b5	cxb5
16. axb5	a5

This is the pawn formation that Black envisioned after 14. ... b6. There are still no open files, but now White can play Nd5 and by using his pawn advantage in the center, he can gradually force lines open.

17. Nd5	Qc5
18. c4	

Diagram 220

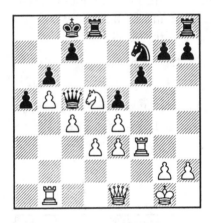

Now the knight will be dominant in the center. White prepares to open the position with d3-d4 and c4-c5.

18. ...	Ng5
19. Rf2	Ne6
20. Qc3	Rd7
21. Rd1	

Stage one: Preparations for d3-d4 are complete.

Diagram 221

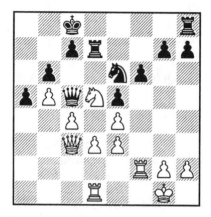

21. ...	Kb7
22. d4	Qd6
23. Rc2	

Diagram 222

Stage two: White is ready for c4-c5.

23. ...	exd4
24. exd4	Nf4
25. c5	Nxd5

Black is lost, but play continued for a few more moves.

26. exd5	Qxd5
27. c6+	Kb8
28. cxd7	Qxd7
29. d5	Re8
30. d6	cxd6
31. Qc6	Black resigns.

Open lines at any cost

Diagram 223
Tchigorin — Pillsbury
St. Petersburg, 1895

1. e4 e5 2. Nf3 Nc6 3. Bb5 g6 4. Nc3 Bg7 5. d3 Nge7 6. Bg5 f6 7. Be3 a6 8. Ba4 b5 9. Bb3 Na5 10. Qd2 Nxb3 11. axb3 Bb7 12. Bh6 0-0

Here White correctly refrained from playing the routine 13. 0-0, preferring to castle long and use his kingside pawns for attack instead of defense.

13. h4!	**d6**
14. 0-0-0	

White threatens to advance in the center with d3-d4, which Black promptly prevents.

14. ...	c5
15. g4	b4
16. Nb1	a5

Black now has a clear, active plan (advancing ... a5-a4 to open the a-file for attack), but White has made greater progress on the kingside.

Diagram 224

17. Rdg1

White's rooks station themselves on files that will soon be open.

17. ...	a4
18. bxa4	Rxa4
19. Qe3	

Killing two birds with one stone! This move not only opens an escape path for the king via d2, but also creates the possibility of transferring the queen to g3.

Diagram 225

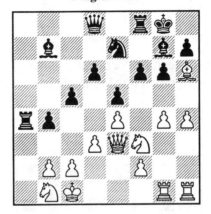

19. ...	Nc6
20. Bxg7	Kxg7
21. g5!	Nd4
22. h5!	Nxf3

Diagram 226

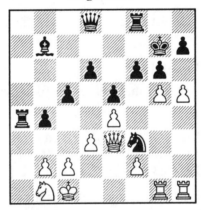

23. hxg6

Opening lines at any cost!

| 23. ... | Nxg1 |
| 24. gxf6+ | Kxf6 |

Or 24. ... Qxf6 25. Qh6+ Kg8 26. Qxh7 mate.

25. gxh7	Ke6
26. Rxg1	Kd7
27. Qh3+	Kc6

Black's king has managed to flee to the queenside (while preserving an extra rook), but White's pawn on h7, together with his active pieces, means that the danger for Black is not over.

28. Qe6	Ra8
29. Rg7	Kb6

Diagram 227

30. Na3!

Another piece joins the attack. Now 30. ... bxa3 fails to 31. Qb3+.

30. ...	Ba6
31. Rd7	Qxd7

Black is forced to give up his queen.

32. Qxd7	Rad8
33. Qg7	bxa3
34. bxa3	c4
35. d4	Rxf2?

A mistake in a difficult position. It was relatively better to keep control over h8.

Diagram 228

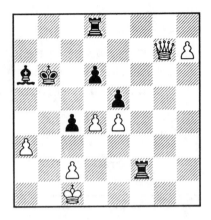

36. h8=Q	Rxh8
37. Qxh8	Rf1+
38. Kb2	exd4
39. Qxd4+	

White has a decisive material advantage.

Diagram 229

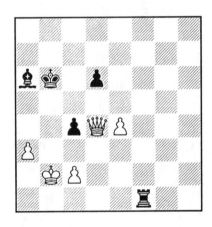

39. ...	Kc7
40. a4	Rf7
41. a5	Kc8

42. Qxd6	Rb7+
43. Kc3	Bb5
44. a6	Rc7
45. a7	**Black resigns.**

In the following related example, White's attack arrives first because of a timely sacrifice to expose Black's king.

Diagram 230
Rubinstein — Teichmann
Match, 1908

1. d4 d5 2. c4 e6 3. Nc3 Nf6 4. Bg5 Nbd7 5. e3 Be7 6. Nf3 0-0 7. Qc2 b6 8. cxd5 exd5 9. Bd3 Bb7 10. 0-0-0 c5

11. h4	c4

Probably expecting the "normal" 12. Be2, when White's lineup on the b1-h7 diagonal is interrupted.

12. Bf5!	Re8
13. Bxf6	Nxf6
14. g4	Bd6
15. g5	Ne4
16. h5	

An exemplary pawn duo.

Diagram 231

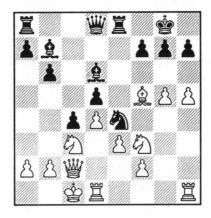

16. ...	Qe7
17. Rdg1	a6

Black prepares counterplay by advancing his b-pawn to b4, but it is already too late. White is ready to open lines on the kingside and to bring his rooks into play.

Diagram 232

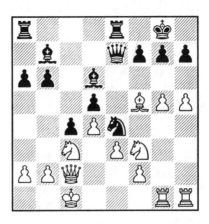

18. Bxh7+!

White gets nowhere without this sacrifice since 16. g6 fxg6 17. hxg6 h6 brings the attack to a halt.

| 18. ... | Kxh7 |
| 19. g6+ | Kg8 |

Bad for Black is 19. ... fxg6 20. Nxe4 dxe4 21. Ng5+.

| 20. Nxe4 | dxe4 |

Not 20. ... Qxe4? 21. gxf7+ Kxf7 22. Ng5+.

21. h6!

Now Black has no available forces to oppose White on the g- and h-files.

Diagram 233

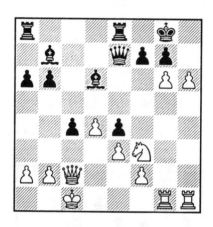

21. ...	f6
22. hxg7	exf3
23. Rh8+	Kxg7
24. Rh7+	Kg8
25. Qf5	c3
26. Rxe7	**Black resigns.**

It is the opponent's pawn weaknesses that make a successful pawn storm possible — the most common plan of attack when the kings are castled on opposite sides. When White castles long and Black castles short, for example, the placement of a pawn at g6 (or b3) encourages the opponent to advance with h2-h4-h5 (or ... a7-a5-a4), either sacrificing or exchanging the h-pawn (or a-pawn), so that a file will be opened for the attack.

The following examples illustrate the theme of *attack on the h- and a-files when there is opposite-side castling*. This kind of attack is common in modern openings such as the Saemisch Attack in the King's Indian Defense, the Yugoslav Attack in the Dragon Sicilian, and various lines in the Pirc and Modern Defenses. In these and many other openings, Black plays ... g7-g6 and ... Bf8-g7, placing his dark-squared bishop on the long a1-h8 diagonal in a maneuver known as a "fianchetto" (FEE-an-KET-to). Often White will play Be3 (or Bg5) followed by Qd2, so that at a favorable moment, White can play Bh6 and Bxg7, exchanging the fianchettoed bishop, which is Black's most important kingside defender.

Attacking the fianchetto

Diagram 234
Spassky — Evans
Varna Olympiad, 1962

1. d4 Nf6 2. c4 g6 3. Nc3 Bg7 4. e4 d6 5. f3 c6 6. Be3 a6

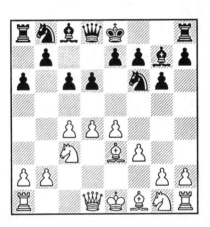

White intends to attack on the kingside, where Black must castle sooner or later. Since it is unlikely that either side will make a major breakthrough in the center, the logical plan for Black is to undertake operations on the other side of the board.

| 7. Qd2 | b5 |
| 8. 0-0-0 | |

The right decision. If Black does not capture the pawn at c4 he will make no progress.

| 8. ... | bxc4 |
| 9. Bxc4 | |

Having delayed the development of the bishop on f1, White loses no time in recapturing on c4.

| 9. ... | 0-0 |
| 10. h4 | |

White chooses a very direct method of attack.

| 10. ... | d5 |

Diagram 235

Countering a flank attack with a central counter-thrust is a natural and logical plan. But right now it would be better to play 10. ... h5 and slow down the pawn storm, even though it weakens the kingside slightly.

| **11. Bb3** | **dxe4** |

Now it is too late for 11. ... h5 because of 12. e5 Ne8 13. g4 hxg4 14. h5, when the opening of the h-file will be fatal for Black because of the absence of a knight on f6.

12. h5!	exf3

Bad for Black is 12. ... Nxh5 13. g4 Nf6 14. Bh6. White need not be concerned about losing kingside pawns since their absence only opens lines and helps his attack.

13. hxg6	hxg6
14. Bh6	fxg2
15. Rh4	

Diagram 236

This position confirms the correctness of White's plan: The h-file is open and available for use by White's heavy artillery. The next stage for White is to exchange the dark-squared defender at g7 to further weaken Black's kingside and also to prevent any potential counterplay along the a1-h8 diagonal. Black cannot block the h-file with 15. ... Nh5 since the simple sacrifice 16. Rxh5 gxh5 17. Qg5 wins for White.

15. ...	Ng4
16. Bxg7	Kxg7
17. Qxg2	

The threat is 18. Rxg4. Note that 17. ... Ne3? is not possible because of 18. Qh2 Rh8 19. Rxh8 Qxh8 20. Qe5+, winning the knight on e3.

17. ...	Nh6
18. Nf3	Nf5
19. Rh2	

Diagram 237

| 19. ... | Qd6 |

On 19. ... Ne3 White replies 20. Qg5, and on 19. ... Rh8 20. Bxf7! is very strong.

20. Ne5	Nd7
21. Ne4	Qc7
22. Rdh1	

Diagram 238

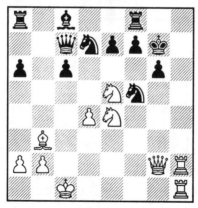

White completely dominates the h-file, and all of his pieces are very active. White's attacking plan has succeeded, and the end is near.

22. ...	Rg8
23. Rh7+	Kf8
24. Rxf7+	Ke8
25. Qxg6	Nxe5
26. Rf8+	**Black resigns.**

This game (Spassky—Evans) brilliantly demonstrated how to open the h-file to get to the Black king.

Diagram 239
Boleslavsky — Geller
Zurich, 1953

Position after Black's 10th move

11. g4

The opening phase of the game has just ended, and White immediately starts to advance his pawns on the kingside. His main idea is to play h2-h4-h5 to open the h-file for his heavy pieces.

The position is somewhat similar to the previous one. In our opinion this position is slightly better for Black because he has good chances of creating a counterattack on the c-file.

We should pay attention to White's opportunities for playing Bh6 with the idea of exchanging Black's bishop on g7. Is this kind of exchange useful to the attacking side? Yes, because by getting the fianchettoed bishop out of the way, White weakens the position of Black's king.

Then why did White not play 11. Bh6? Because Black would answer 11. ... Nxd4 12. Bxg7 Nxf3 winning material. And if first White exchanges knights with 11. Nxc6 then after 11. ... bxc6 Black has more control in the center and also gains the possibility of attacking the weak b2-square on the open b-file.

11. ...   Rc8

Should Black try to stop the White pawns with 11. ... h5?

No — 11. ... h5 weakens the kingside and does not prevent the opening of a file. White would continue 12. gxh5 Nxh5 13. Rg1, after which the nasty threat of 14. Nf5! would give White a very strong attack.

12. Kb1

This is a standard move in this kind of position. Often the a2-pawn needs another protector, especially after Black plays ... Qa5. But in this position there is no immediate need for Kb1, so 12. h4 deserves attention.

12. ...   Ne5
13. h4

After 13. Bh6 play might continue 13. ... Bxh6 14. Qxh6 Rxc3 15. bxc3 d5, when as compensation for the Exchange Black would have the initiative and White's castled position would be seriously weakened.

13. ...   b5

It is not easy for Black to create counterplay. After 13. ... Nc4 14. Bxc4 Rxc4, White would continue his plan with 15. h5. Black's last move prepares ... Nc4 and in case of an exchange Black would be able to take on c4 with the pawn, and then concentrate his attack on the b2-pawn. Of course Black can also move the b-pawn forward.

Diagram 240

The Black pawn on b5 is attacked three times. Could White just take it?

GM David Bronstein in his comments about this game wrote: "It would be insane to take the pawn on b5."

We agree with the spirit of Bronstein's comment — 13. ... b5 is a typical positional sacrifice, and that is why Geller did not spend his time on lengthy calculations prior to making this move. He just used his intuition and experience with these types of positions. Again, let's check some sample lines:

(1) 14. Bxb5 Bxb5 15. Ncxb5 a6 16. Na3 (if 16. Nc3, then 16. ... Nc4 and 17. ... Qb6) 16. ... Rb8 and Black has a good position for the pawn — the threat is 17. ... Nxf3 18. Nxf3 Nxe4.

(2) 14. Ncxb5 Rb8 (with the threat 15. ... Nxf3 and taking aim at the b2-square).

14. Bh6

Stronger was 14. h5, avoiding for a while the Exchange sacrifice that occurred in the game.

14. ...   Bxh6
15. Qxh6

White has created some real weaknesses in Black's position. However, by sacrificing the Exchange Black gains the initiative.

| 15. ... | Rxc3 |
| 16. bxc3 | Qa5 |

Diagram 241

17. Qe3

If 17. Kb2 then Black continues the attack with 17. ... b4.

| 17. ... | Qa3 |
| 18. h5 | |

Too late — the players' roles have completely reversed. Now Black's queenside attack is the more dangerous one, and White is the defender.

18. ...   b4

After 18. ... Rc8 White can defend with 19. Nb3—for example, 19. ... a5 20. Be2 a4 21. Qc1 Qxc1+ 22. Nxc1 Rxc3 23. Nd3. Generally speaking, after the exchange of queens Black's attack will evaporate, and an extra Exchange in a simplified position starts to play a big role. In the endgame one pawn might not turn out to be enough material compensation for the Exchange.

19. Qc1

If 19. Nb3, then 19. ... a5, after which White can't play 20. cxb4 because of 20. ... a4 21. Qc1 Qxb4. By sacrificing a pawn, White aims to consolidate the position of his king.

19. ...	**Qxc3**
20. Qb2	**Rc8**

Diagram 242

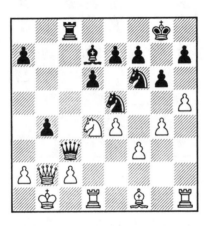

Black thinks, too optimistically, that his chances in this ending are fairly good.

21. hxg6	**Qxb2+**
22. Kxb2	**hxg6**
23. a3?	

An oversight. Instead 23. Be2 deserved attention, intending to follow up with Ra1 and a2-a3 to open files for the rooks.

23. ...	**bxa3+**
24. Kxa3	**Nxf3**

This is what White missed: He is losing a pawn, and with the loss of this pawn the whole pawn chain on the kingside is destroyed.

Diagram 243

25. Nxf3	Rc3+
26. Kb2	Rxf3

The additional material losses that follow are inevitable.

27. e5   **Nxg4**

Of course not 27. ... dxe5 28. g5.

28. Be2

The move 28. exd6 is bad because of 28. ... Nf2—for example, 29. Rd2 (or 29. Rd4 e5) 29. ... Nxh1 30. dxe7 Ba4.

Diagram 244

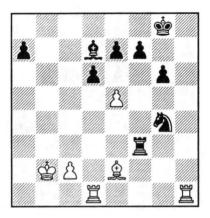

28. ...	Rf2
29. Bxg4	Bxg4
30. Rdf1	

After 30. Ra1 dxe5, Black's strong pawns should decide the game in his favor.

30. ...	Rxf1
31. Rxf1	dxe5
32. c4	

After 32. Ra1 Be6, Black would simply advance his f- and g-pawns.

Diagram 245

The finish was **32. ... Kf8 33. Ra1 Bf3 34. c5 g5 35. Rxa7 g4 36. Ra3 Ke8.** (Of course not 36. ... e4 because of 37. c6 — alertness is necessary up to the last moment!) **37. Kc1 f5 38. Kd2 f4 39. Ra6 g3 40. Ke1 Be4 White resigns.**

We have seen a couple of examples where a pawn attack was launched on a weakened castled position. The potential weakenings associated with the moves h6 (h3) and g6 (g3) are typical and are very common in practice.

The next example shows a similar attack on the a-file in which the White king perishes because of exploitable weaknesses in his pawn cover.

Invasion on the a-file

Gereban — Geller
Budapest, 1952

1. e4 c5 2. Nf3 d6 3. d4 cxd4 4. Nxd4 Nf6 5. Nc3 a6 6. h3 Nc6 7. g4 Nxd4 8. Qxd4 e5 9. Qd3 Be7 10. Bg2 Be6 11. b3 0-0 12. Bb2 b5 13. 0-0-0

Diagram 246

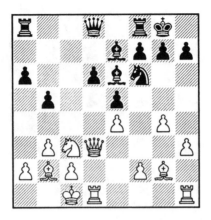

13. ...	b4
14. Ne2	a5

Black's intentions are clear: He will advance his a-pawn, because the position of White's b3-pawn will allow the second player to open additional lines on the queenside. White must find some type of counterplay — if he does nothing, Black's threats on the queenside will soon be overwhelming.

15. f4	Nd7

Black mobilizes his reserves, bringing all his forces together for the assault.

16. f5	Nc5

This "in-between" move saves the bishop, which had no retreat square. Now d7 and c8 are vacant.

17. Qf3

Diagram 247

What would you do now? Take a moment to try to figure out Black's next move for yourself.

17. ...	**a4!**

Of course! Black doesn't want to waste a single tempo in his attack. Capturing the bishop is bad, since 18. fxe6 fxe6 opens the f-file for Black's rook with gain of time.

In situations like this, with sharp play for both sides, the most important factor is gaining the initiative. Most players would stop analyzing after 18. fxe6 fxe6 19. Qg3 (19. Qe3? Bg5 wins the queen) 19. ... Bh4, sensing that gaining the initiative was worth the material investment. This intuition would be correct since after 20. Qh2 Rf2 21. Rhe1 Bg5+, White will soon be mated; for example, 22. Kb1 axb3 23. axb3 Qa5 24. Nc1 Bxc1 25. Kxc1 Nxb3+ 26. cxb3 Qa1+!! 27. Bxa1 Rxa1 mate.

18. h4	**axb3**
19. axb3	**Ra2!**

Invasion! This threatens ... Qa5 followed by ... Rxb2 and ... Qa3+, after which the remaining rook comes to a8.

Diagram 248

20. fxe6	fxe6
21. Qe3	Qa5
22. c4	

Diagram 249

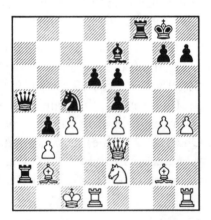

22. ...	Rxb2!

As a result of this latest sacrifice, the last defender is removed. Without pieces for defense, White's king is doomed.

23. Kxb2	Qa3+
24. Kb1	Ra8

Even though he is behind in material overall, Black has a decisive advantage in attacking power on the queenside.

25. Nc1	Qa1+
26. Kc2	

Diagram 250

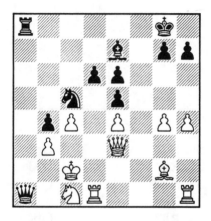

26. ...	Ra2+
27. Nxa2	Qxa2+

Now Black recovers his material investment, with interest. Black's continuing initiative, together with White's numerous weak pawns, is enough to win.

28. Kc1	Nxb3+
29. Qxb3	Qxb3

Diagram 251

30. Rd2	Qc3+
31. Rc2	Qe3+
32. Kb2	Qa3+
33. Kb1	b3
34. Rb2	Qb4
35. g5	

Diagram 252

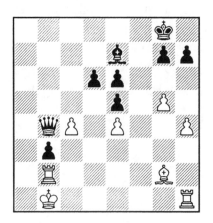

35. ...	Bd8
36. Rc1	Bb6
37. Bh3	Kf8

38. h5	Bd4
39. g6	hxg6
40. hxg6	Ke7

White resigns.

Sometimes in positions with castling on opposite sides the pawn storm does not manage to open files against the enemy king, but instead creates weak squares in the opponent's pawn structure. The following game shows the exploitation of an open diagonal.

Extending a diagonal

Diagram 253
Razuvayev — Kapengut
Dubna, 1970

1. b3	e5
2. Bb2	d6
3. e3	Nd7

4. f4

Trying to open the diagonal for his bishop.

4. ...	Be7
5. Nc3	exf4
6. exf4	Bf6

With this move, Black is trying to neutralize White's strong bishop at b2.

7. Qf3		Ne7
8. 0-0-0		0-0
9. g4		

White starts his pawn advance, with the idea of weakening the dark squares around his opponent's king, and extending the reach of his bishop on b2.

Diagram 254

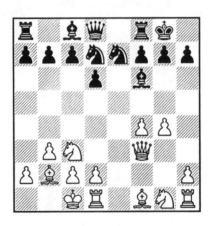

9. ...		Nc6
10. g5		Bd4
11. Nge2		Nb6
12. h4		f5
13. h5		d5
14. Qd3		Bc5
15. h6		

Diagram 255

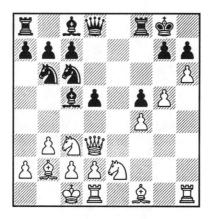

White's pawns have reached their target squares, weakening the dark squares near the Black king along the a1-h8 diagonal.

15. ...	g6
16. a3	Qe7
17. b4	Bxb4

Black can't just sit still and allow White to keep attacking, so he launches a counterattack by sacrificing a piece.

| 18. axb4 | Nxb4 |
| 19. Qd4! | |

Any other Queen move would lead to an inferior position for White.

| 19. ... | c5 |

Diagram 256

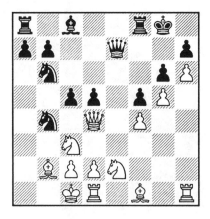

20. Qh8+!!	Kxh8

Creating a discovered check that unleashes the power of the bishop at b2.

21. Nxd5+	Kg8
22. Nxe7+	Kf7
23. Nxc8	**Black resigns.**

Now let's analyse an attack against a strong castled position. We will consider a classic example where White has a pawn majority on the kingside, while Black has a queenside majority.

Kingside majority

Diagram 257
Alekhine — Marshall
Baden-Baden, 1925

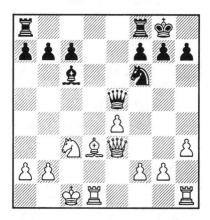

Position after Black's 15th move

White's pawns can immediately move forward with gain of time. Black, however, cannot activate his queenside pawn majority.

| 16. f4 | Qe6 |

Instead 16. ... Qa5 would be followed by 17. e5, and if 17. ... Nd5 then 18. Nxd5 Bxd5 19. Bxh7+.

| 17. e5 | Rfe8 |

Taking the pawn on g2 would be suicidal for Black, because after 18. Rhg1 or 18. f5, White's attack would be unstoppable.

| **18. Rhe1** | **Rad8** |

This leads to a forced win for White. A lesser evil would be 18. ... Nd7 19. g4.

Diagram 258

19. f5	Qe7
20. Qg5	Nd5
21. f6	Qf8
22. Bc4	Nxc3

On 22. ... h6 White wins after 23. fxg7.

23. Rxd8	**Rxd8**

Diagram 259

24. fxg7

Also winning is 24. e6, with the threats 25. e7 and 25. exf7+.
The choice is just a matter of taste.

24. ...	Nxa2+
25. Kb1	

On 25. Bxa2 Black would answer 25. ... Qc5+ 26. Kb1 Rd7.

25. ...	Qe8

If 25. ... Nc3+, then simply 26. bxc3.

26. e6	Be4+

Diagram 260

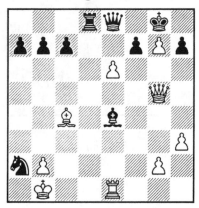

27. Ka1

This is the easiest way, but the bishop could also be taken:
27. Rxe4 Rd1+ 28. Kc2 Qa4+ 29. b3.

27. ...	f5
28. e7+	Rd5
29. Qf6	Qf7
30. e8=Q+	Black resigns.

White won because he correctly gained the initiative by advancing his pawn majority on the kingside, giving him the possibility of leading an energetic attack. Black did not have an equivalent source of counterplay.

Exercises

1

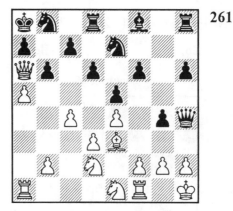

261

White to move

2

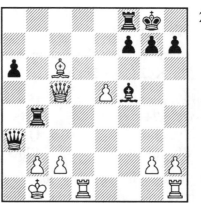

262

White to move

3

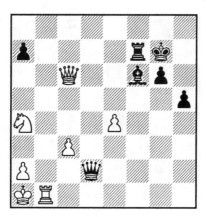

263

Black to move

4

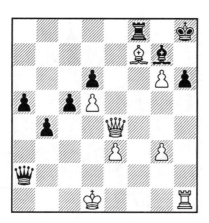

264

White to move

5

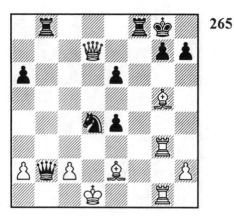

265

White to move

6

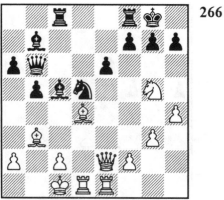

266

White to move

7

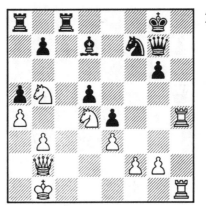

267

White to move

8

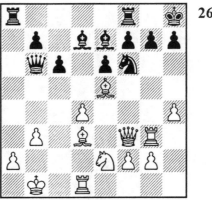

268

White to move

9

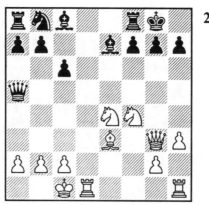

269

White to move

10

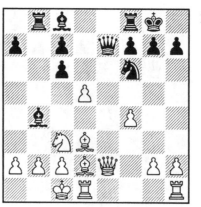

270

Black to move

11

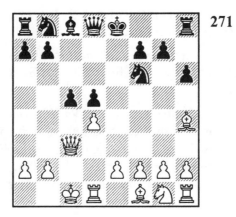

271

Black to move

12

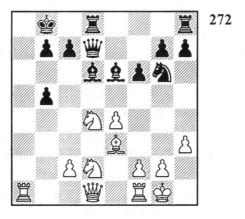

272

White to move

Solutions

1. Janowsky — Amstman, Paris, 1892. **1. Qxa7+ Kxa7 2. axb6+ Kb7 3. Ra7+ Kc6 4. Rxc7 mate**.

2. *Westerinen — Loikkanen, Finland, 1963.* Black is closing in for the kill, but White can get there first with **1. Qxf8+ Kxf8 2. Rd8+ Ke7 3. Re8 mate**.

3. *Satianatan — Krupin, New York, 1996.* When there is play on both sides of the board, a bishop can be a very powerful piece. **1. ... Qd7!** **2. Qc4.** (If 2. Qxd7 Rxd7 the ending is winning for Black because of his connected passed pawns.) **2. ... Qxa4!** and **Black won**. If 3. Qxa4 Bxc3+ 4. Rb2 Rf1+ and mate next move. This beautiful finish occurred in the under 2000 section — you don't have to be a master to play great chess!

4. Rotstein — Katalymov, USSR, 1952. Everybody has to get into the act. **1. Rxh6+ Bxh6 2. g7+! Kxg7.** (Or 2. ... Bxg7 3. Qh4+ and 4. Qxh6 mate) **3. Qg6+ Kh8 4. Qxh6 mate**.

5. *Westerinen — Sigurjonsson, New York, 1978.* White must act quickly since his own king is in danger. **1. Qxg7+ Kxg7 2. Bd8+! Kh8.** (If 2. ... Kf7 3. Bh5 mate, or 2. ... Kh6 3. Rh3 mate.) **3. Rg8+! Rxg8 4. Bf6+ Rg7 5. Bxg7+ Kg8 6. Bxd4+ Kf7 7. Bxb2** and **White won**.

6. *Ciocaltea — Sandor, Varna, 1969.* How do you bring more forces into the attack? **1. Qh5 h6 2. Rxe6! fxe6 3. Qg6** and White won.

7. *Lubisavlievic — Albano, Ciocco, 1973.* **1. Nd6! Nxd6 2. Rh8+ Qxh8** (or 2. ... Kf7 3. R8h7) **3. Rxh8+ Kxh8 4. Nf5+ Kg8** (or ... Kh7) **5. Qg7 mate**.

8. *Radulov — Stenborg, Helsinki, 1961.* **1. Rxg7! Kxg7 2. Qg4+ Kh8** (2. ... Kh6 3. Qg5 mate) **3. Qe4** with mate on h7 to follow.

9. *Mabs — Alexander, England, 1961.* Everything is ready, but you must finish the job. **1. Rd5! cxd5 2. Nh5 g6 3. Qe5 gxh5 4. Bh6 f6 5.Qxe7** with mate to follow.

10. *Slonim — Riumin, Moscow, 1931.* **1. ... Ba3!** (a la Morphy) **2. Na4** (if 2. Qxe7 then 2. ... Bxb2+ 3. Kb1 Bxc3+ 4. Kc1 Bb2+ 5. Kb1 Ba3+) **2. ... Bxb2+ 3. Nxb2 Qa3 4. Qe5 Re8 5. Qd4 c5 6. Qc3 Qxa2**. (This shows the usual weakness of castling long: The a2 square is not protected!) **7. Be1 Re2!! 8. Bxe2 Ne4** and **White resigned** since he has no defense to checkmate.

11. *Keres — Botvinnik, USSR Championship, 1941.* When White castled long he underestimated the power of opening the c-file. His opponent soon enlightened him: **1. ... g5 2. Bg3 cxd4 3. Qxd4 Nc6 4. Qa4 Bf5.** (Now the king can't run to a1.) **5. e3 Rc8 6. Bd3 Qd7.** (Threatens discovered check.) **7. Kb1 Bxd3+ 8. Rxd3 Qf5 9. e4 Nxe4 10. Ka1** (too late!) **10. ... 0-0** (not 10. ... Nc5 11. Re3+) **11. Rd1 b5 12. Qxb5 Nd4 13. Qd3 Nc2+ 14. Kb1 Nb4** and **White resigned**; for example, 15. Qf3 Nd2+ 16. Ka1 Nc2 mate.

12. *Wahls — Bjarnason, Malmo, 1985.* **1. Ra8+ Kxa8 2. Qa1+ Kb8 3. Qa7+ Kxa7 4. Nc6+ Ka8 5. Ra1+ Ba3 6. Rxa3 mate.** The a-file was like an interstate highway for White's pieces!

Conclusion

After considering these many examples illustrating the attack on the king, we would like to make the following observations.

We think you will agree with us that in chess, an attack is not only a bit of fantasy, a creative work of the imagination, but is also a logical process which makes use of specific chess knowledge and facts, such as the basic elements of combinations and attacking strategems. In this volume, we have concentrated on presenting various broad categories of attacking formations. For a detailed discussion of the most common tactical devices, please see the previous book in this series, *Chess Tactics for the Tournament Player*.

We believe that these basic skills (such as making combinations and recognizing attacking schemes) can be effectively learned.

Our intention was to provide players of intermediate strength with an introduction to the fundamental principles that underlie any successful attack on the king. It is true that positions sometimes arise in which the attack goes outside the classification scheme used in this book. It would not be hard to find games in which some of our general conclusions might not apply. In most cases, however, our general principles will help players to understand more about the ebb and flow of the chess struggle. We emphasize that this book is not intended as a comprehensive theory of attack, and that we have only presented the most basic type of examples as a way of introducing the subject. Our next book in the *Comprehensive Chess Course* series, *Chess Strategy for the Tournament Player*, continues to discuss the relationship between tactical devices and the overall strategic content of the position.

It is important to point out that attacks and combinations are not possible in every position. Recall the advice of Steinitz: Attacks should be prepared carefully, through the accumulation of small advantages. First of all, the pieces should be developed quickly and efficiently, either by occupying the center or at least establishing some control over it. Successful control of the center will guarantee that you have more space, more maneuverability for your pieces, and thus the preconditions for a successful attack. By considering the plans and opportunities for both sides and making an objective evaluation of the position, you will be able to choose the correct plan and determine the right direction for developing an attack. However, as we have already seen, a decisive combination is possible only when the opponent's position is weakened, or when the harmony between the enemy's pieces is disrupted.

Keep in mind that by deploying your forces actively, seizing greater space, opening lines, bringing superior force to the main battleground, and creating weaknesses in the enemy camp, you can guide your ship of attack into the port of victory. Imagination, bravery, practice, and acquiring new knowledge and experience guarantee you happy sailing!

Remember: If you have a temporary advantage in development or mobility, you must attack or else you will lose your advantage.

To this general rule, we can add an important corollary. *If you believe that you have the better position, you must be able to state why that is so in words.* Only when you have a firm grasp of why you stand better (if that is the case) can you move on to the more concrete task of implementing the attack. If you can't say why you stand better, you probably don't!

The practical player must constantly be on the alert for opportunities to recognize the sort of advantages that may lead to a successful attack. To reinforce this principle, the next time you are conducting a winning attack, stop for a moment and notice how many of these smaller advantages are present in the position just prior to the decisive blow.

You will undoubtedly want to return to some of the examples and conclusions about each general type of position. These examples will help to guide you as you conduct your own attacks in tournament and casual games.

By increasing your understanding of various attacking methods, by recognizing the wisdom of accumulating smaller advantages before launching an attack, and by learning how to make combinations, you will soon be feeling more confident as a player. As your mastery of these principles increases, so will your tournament successes.

Index of Games

Games appear twice, indexed by both White and Black players.

Grandmaster Sam Palatnik

(right) is an internationally famous chess instructor. He was for many years the captain of the Ukrainian squad that won medals from bronze up to gold in the chess Olympics and World Team championships.

Additionally, Palatnik served as trainer for some of the world's leading individual players, such as GM Vassily Ivanchuk. In honor of Palatnik's achievements in educating several generations of grandmasters, Ukraine awarded him the rank of "Honored Coach."

GM Palatnik has earned an impressive list of victories. He was 1979 USSR Team Champion, World Student Champion (1974-1976), and World Open Champion (1991). He was twice European Cup Champion (1976-1979) and seven times Tennessee State Champion (1994-2001).

GM Palatnik currently serves as Head Instructor of the Memphis City School Chess Project, where he provides teacher and coach training and consultation, and is a highlight of MCS' chess camps. He also provides chess exhibitions, as well as group and individual lessons in person, byEmail or by telephone. For details call (901) 725-7534 or Email Palatnik@earthlink.net.

Palatnik is also a popular writer of several of the best-selling chess books in America.

Olga Palatnik (above left) was born in Kiev in 1981, and she has lived in the US since 1994. She recently graduated from American University in Washington, DC. Olga Palatnik currently ranks among the top 50 women chess players in the United States.

International Grandmaster
Lev Alburt

Grandmaster Lev Alburt was born in Orenburg, Russia, on August 21, 1945. For many years, he lived in Odessa, a Ukrainian city located on the Black Sea. A three-time champion of the Ukraine (1972-74), he became European Cup champion in 1976. In 1979, while in West Germany for a chess competition, he defected and came to the US, making his home in New York City.

Mentored by three-time World Champion and eminent teacher Mikhail Botvinnik, Grandmaster Alburt first taught chess in the Soviet Union. He is now in the forefront of the innovative movement known as "the new chess pedagogy," which seeks new ways to teach chess to both beginners and more advanced players, regardless of their ages or backgrounds. GM Alburt's *Comprehensive Chess Course* is one of the most important works of this movement.

GM Alburt has won the U.S. Championship an impressive three times—in 1984, 1985, and 1990. He is known as the "Grandmaster of chess teachers." He is the only top-echelon GM to devote his career to teaching those below master strength.

Currently, GM Alburt is a popular columnist for *Chess Life*, a best-selling chess author, and a renowned teacher. He provides lessons through-the-mail, over-the-telephone, and face-to-face. Write to GM Alburt at P.O. Box 534, Gracie Station, New York, NY 10028, or call him at (212) 794-8706.

The right 7 books can make you a Chess Champ!

You want to improve quickly, and you have limited time to study chess. That's why *GM Lev Alburt* co-wrote and published the Comprehensive Chess Course. *Seven books that contain only what it takes to win. Seven books that save you years of random reading and hit-and-miss improvement. Based on the once-secret Russian lesson plans used to produce the long line of World Champions still at the top today, CCC now takes you from beginner to master.*

"I've been reading chess books for 40 years. Lev taught me basic things that no one else ever taught me. He is a brilliant teacher, and his books capture that brilliance."
— Charles Murray, author of *What It Means to Be a Libertarian*

"GM Lev Alburt offers the once-secret Russian method of chess training."
— 13th World Champion Garry Kasparov

Co-authored with Roman Pelts, Sam Palatnik and Nickolay Krogius,

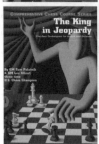

Improve Faster Than You Ever Thought Possible!

with Personal Instruction from 3-time U.S. Champ GM Lev Alburt!

As a chess teacher, my job is to provide my students quick, steady, and noticeable improvement, without wasting their valuable time. After discussing your chess and analyzing your games, I'll design the most effective, personalized study program for you—based on the same, proven, Russian-developed system that led to half a century of world champions. *It does work.*

Through-the-mail lessons start at $80/hour. Over-the-telephone and face-to-face lessons are also available. In the long run, these lessons can save you thousands of dollars and hundreds of hours. You'll escape buying an untold number of books not right for you, and you'll avoid wasting time on false leads.

Even a single lesson can help you reassess your chess and put you on the right track to major improvement—and winning more chess games!

Reach your full potential.
Contact me today to schedule your first lesson!

Write to:
GM Lev Alburt,
P.O. Box 534, Gracie Station,
New York, NY 10028-0005
or
Call me at (212) 794-8706

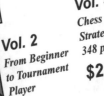